THE
BEST
BRITISH
POETRY
2013

◊ ◊ ◊

AHREN WARNER was born in 1986. His first collection, *Confer* (Bloodaxe, 2011), was both a Poetry Book Society Recommendation and shortlisted for the Forward Prize for Best First Collection. His poems have appeared widely in magazines and anthologies and he has also published a pocket-book, *Re:,* with Donut Press. He was awarded an Eric Gregory Award in 2010 and an Arts Foundation Fellowship in 2012. His second collection of poems, *Pretty*, was published in 2013 and is also a Poetry Book Society Recommendation. He is poetry editor of *Poetry London*.

RODDY LUMSDEN (born 1966) is a Scottish poet, who was born in St Andrews. He has published six collections of poetry, a number of chap-books and a collection of trivia, as well as editing a generational anthology of British and Irish poets of the 1990s and 2000s, *Identity Parade*. He lives in London where he teaches for The Poetry School. He has done editing work on several prize-winning poetry collections and edited the Pilot series of chapbooks by poets under 30 for tall-lighthouse. He is organiser and host of the monthly reading series BroadCast in London. In 2010, he was appointed as Poetry Editor for Salt.

THE
BEST
BRITISH
POETRY
2013

◇　◇　◇

AHREN WARNER, *Editor*

RODDY LUMSDEN, *Series Editor*

CROMER

PUBLISHED BY SALT

12 Norwich Road, Cromer, Norfolk NR27 0AX United Kingdom

Printed in Great Britain by Clays Ltd, St Ives plc

Typeset in Bembo 10.5 / 12

ISBN 978 1 90773 55 6 paperback

1 3 5 7 9 8 6 4 2

CONTENTS

Foreword by Roddy Lumsden   vii
Introduction by Ahren Warner   viii

Rachael Allen, 'Sunday'   1
Emily Berry, 'Arlene's House'   3
Liz Berry, 'Bird'   5
Patrick Brandon, 'The Spirit of Geometry'   7
James Brookes, 'Amen to Artillery'   8
Sam Buchan-Watts, 'Nose to Tail'   9
Hayley Buckland, 'Supper'   10
Harry Burke, 'realspace'   11
John Burnside, 'At the Entering of the New Year'   13
Matthew Caley, 'My Beloved'   16
Niall Campbell, 'On Eriskay'   17
Ian Cartland, 'Six Winters'   18
Melanie Challenger, 'The Daffodil'   23
Kayo Chingonyi, from 'calling a spade a spade'   24
John Clegg, 'Figtree'   25
David Constantine, 'Foxes, rain'   26
Emily Critchley, 'Some Curious Thing II'   27
Claire Crowther, 'Trompe l'oeil'   36
Francine Elena, 'Ode to a 1980s Baton Twirling World Champion'   37
Menna Elfyn, 'Babysitting in the Crematorium'   38
    'Carco yn y Crem'   39
Leontia Flynn, 'MacNeice's Mother'   40
Charlotte Geater, 'avoid using the word "pussy"'   41
Dai George, 'Seven Rounds with Bill's Ghost'   43
Matthew Gregory, 'A Room in Taiwan, 2010'   46
Philip Gross, 'The Works'   47
David Harsent, 'Effaced'   49
Stuart Henson, 'The Builder'   50
Wayne Holloway-Smith, 'Poem in Which'   51
Sarah Howe, 'Scrying: turpentine'   52
A.B. Jackson, from 'Natural History'   54
Andrew Jamison, 'What I'll Say When I Get Back'   55
Alan Jenkins, 'Sea-Music'   56
Chris McCabe, 'The Alchemist'   59
John McCullough, '!'   61
Patrick McGuinness, 'Doors and Windows of Wallonia'   62

Edward Mackay, 'Afterword'   64
Andrew McMillan, 'if it wasn't for the nights'   65
Kona Macphee, 'Mind'   66
Allison McVety, 'Finlandia'   67
D.S. Marriott, 'The Redeemers'   69
Glyn Maxwell, 'Christmas Seven Times Seven'   71
Christopher Middleton, 'The Ghosting Of Paul Celan'   73
Kate Miller, 'Salvage'   75
Helen Mort, 'Admit you feel like all the ice skates in Brazil'   76
Alistair Noon, 'from "Earth Records", 27'   77
Richard O'Brien, 'So Much Will Waste'   78
Sean O'Brien, 'Thirteen O'Clocks'   79
Richard Osmond, 'The Well'   84
Ruth Padel, from 'The Okazaki Fragments'   85
Rebecca Perry, 'Pow'   88
Pascale Petit, 'Sainte-Chapelle'   89
Heather Phillipson, 'Rumination on 25mm of Cotton'   91
Jody Porter, 'Girl at the World's End'   92
Kate Potts, 'Thirty-three'   93
Sam Riviere, 'No Touching'   94
Robin Robertson, 'Finding the Keys'   95
Sophie Robinson, 'nsfw'   96
Charlotte Runcie, 'Lothian Road, Saturday Night'   98
Declan Ryan, 'From Alun Lewis'   99
Fiona Sampson, 'The Revenant'   100
Camellia Stafford, 'I will stay at home and talk on the telephone'   102
Chloe Stopa-Hunt, 'The Paris Poems'   103
Michael Symmons Roberts, 'After a Line by George Seferis'   104
George Szirtes, 'Songlines'   106
Helen Tookey, 'Portrait of a Young Woman'   107
Tim Turnbull, 'Fetish'   108
Mark Waldron, 'Collaboration'   109
Nerys Williams, 'The Thirteen Club'   110

Contributors' Notes and Comments   113
List of Magazines   151
Acknowledgements   153

FOREWORD

by Roddy Lumsden

◊ ◊ ◊

The poems presented in this volume were selected from UK-based poetry magazines, literary journals and online publications issued between spring 2012 and spring 2013. The main purpose of this volume is to celebrate the thriving scene of literary magazines and the developing sphere of literary sites online. For the past year, Ahren Warner and I have been reading these publications as they appeared, seeking poems which we felt should be reproduced here. Though I made recommendations, the choices were Ahren's, as this year's Guest Editor. The format of the book owes a debt to *The Best American Poetry* series of anthologies which was founded in 1988. Similar volumes appear each year in Canada, Australia and Ireland. For the third year in succession, *Poetry London* is the publication with most poems featured. It should be noted that these selections were made before Ahren Warner recently became Poetry Editor of that journal.

INTRODUCTION

by Ahren Warner

◇ ◇ ◇

How does one choose the 'best' poem? Even worse, how can one choose around seventy 'best' poems from the many hundreds published in magazines, newspapers and e-zines over the past year?[1]

I ask this question, having purportedly done such a thing, precisely because it seems – in so many ways – an absurd thing to do. For a start, I'm not sure what 'best' means. When it comes down to it, and in this context, doesn't it really mean: seventy-odd poems that *I* really like?

I hope not.

Indeed, it seems rather dubious that a book of my own favourite poems would merit a title such as *Best British Poetry*. For a start, there are poems that I enjoy, some of them perhaps included here, which are technically flawed. On this note, there are also poems included here that I do not particularly 'enjoy', but that – precisely because of their technical brilliance – I have felt fit to include.

And now, I am reminded [*cue appropriate tone of grandeur*] of what T.S. Eliot wrote [*yawn*] in To Criticize the Critic, i.e. that 'in my earlier criticism . . . I was implicitly defending the sort of poetry that I and my friends wrote.' Well, I don't write like David Harsent – though I often wish I had his gift for turning a truly muscular line – nor, in fact, do I write like Emily Critchley (though, again, if I managed to toe the same line between lyric affect and Modernist inheritance, I'd be very happy). So, it can't be that either.

I guess, when it comes down to it (and putting it bluntly), I have chosen seventy-ish poems that seem to me to be *important* [*cue heckling*].

---

[1] As an aside, are there seventy *really* good poems published in any given year?

There are, of course, poems that I have been unable to include in this anthology, but which I believe to be *important* (Denise Riley, for example, published a poem better than most, though felt it not yet good enough to be republished.)[2]

Despite, then, such various and inevitable exceptions, I have attempted to choose poems, as I've said, that seem of *import*. Indeed, I'll say it again. I think all of the poems included here are *important* (yes, probably more important than those I have not chosen). It's probably worth repeating such a statement, I think, if only because it is the kind of statement that is, these days, rarely heard.

It is not, here, that I want to offer up a purposely contentious editorial (indeed, the editorial included in a particular, rather recent 'young poets' anthology shows how wrong that can go . . .), but simply that – in an attempt at honesty, rather than the usual editorial bumph – I think it's worth articulating the (perhaps simplistic) motivation for what follows with as much clarity as possible.

So, I think the poems here are important and, while we're at it, that – simply by their existence as genuine artworks, what Adorno (in, perhaps, a linguistically post-Kantian vein) might have called their 'mere' existence[3] – they are indices of the importance of poetry itself.[4]

Whether it is the exquisite nature of Sean O'Brien's line breaks, the post-Beckettian self-inquisition offered up by Mark Waldron (a poet, incidentally, writing consistently better than virtually any other at the moment) or the flawless lyricism of Rachael Allen's contemporary excavations, these poems seem to me to be valuable contributions to the art form. As such they deserve to be read and re-read.

There is little more to be said, I think.[5]

Yet, I can't, I'm afraid, let this editorial close without noting that it will be the last time this annual compendium is published by a company still in the business of publishing what, in a certain unattractive jargon, are called 'single author collections' or, indeed, publishing what most people call poetry. Such things do not make money, apparently[6] anthologies do.

---

[2] Riley's 'Nine Blindfolded Songs' can be found in the first issue of *Snow*. Like most of Riley's work, it is exceptional.

[3] Yes, I do indeed hate myself a little for this smugly oblique reference to Theodor W. Adorno. And, yet, I also genuinely believe that page 225 of Hullot-Kentor's translation of Adorno's *Aesthetic Theory*, cross-referenced with Adorno's discussion of negativity in *Negative Dialectics*, would give a better sense of what I'm talking about than yet another paragraph from me.

[4] Along, of course, with fine art, music and, yes, more important than other forms of human activity, like medicine or property development or, indeed, *The Voice*.

[5] Though, I believe I should have mentioned that, after the poems, there are small commentaries on the poems provided by most of the poets. These should be of interest.

[6] Here, I offer a nod towards the wonderful Matthew Caley.

Still, despite the unpleasant circumstances in which an anthology begun in Spring 2012 now comes to print, it is my hope that you will read the poems here and then go on to read (and *buy*) the books that their authors have written or have yet to write. Go on, it will make you a better (if not, perhaps, the *best*) person.

THE
BEST
BRITISH
POETRY
2013

◇ ◇ ◇

Sunday

◊   ◊   ◊

Supermarket Warehouse

This is the ornate layer: in the supermarket warehouse,
boxed children's gardens rocking on a fork-lift truck,
two rats rutting as a closed door would be punched over
and over again (we are locked out: the paddling pools
are torture saying *Florida! Florida! Florida!* forever).
The toys come alive to *Für Elise* as they do in our
combined nightmares, daring each other, spinning on
stray dust leaked into crates, making waves of fur.

Camping in the Supermarket Garden

Outside, the motorway is humming with the night shift
but it is not luminescent or romantic like the glow-gore
of signs in America that say M O T E L. Instead, the
burnt stubble of wildness: low-lying spinney and shrub,
the gradual fallout from car crashes, overage tent-shares
or overage friendship. Unpacked beer for goose-pimpled
men loud with drink, their eyes wide and pale all night.

Home

They go back on Sundays to their Tamblin Avenues and
Hollyhock Gardens, blooming with the fire smell, taking
their shoes off, picking up their tiny babies, having baths.
While sitting, they flick through the catalogue. Watching,
a tight teal or sea-blue orient themed wall frieze, a waist-

belt Millennium hangover; keeping it in. A cat squats and quivers as it craps in the bushes. Now on the quiet estate we are cooking, rest assured things will stay as they are.

from *The White Review*

Arlene's House

◇ ◇ ◇

Arlene lives in our house now and she won't leave.
Her legs are too long for the sofa. I know her cracked
heels like the back of my hand. Since Arlene came
we've forgotten how to manage on our own. My sisters
look to me for guidance. At home we have a doormat
and rugs and a room each but it doesn't matter. Last week
summer fled like it was panic-attacking. Our mood rings
have stopped changing colour. You can get used to
pretty much anything. Arlene just turned up and knew
all the house's tricks, the way the wind sucks doors shut
and the twist in the shower hose. Outside they see her
standing at the window. The neighbours try to ask
if we're all right. She stands at the window and drains
the world until there's nothing to get up for. I miss my baby.
Arlene says he's gone for good. Now I wash my hair
too late in the day and wake with it damp. I go to places
I know and Arlene comes with me, she paints them
and shows me the pictures later. She has a nasty talent.
I stay home more and count the length of each breath.
I count my sisters. Some nights we're too scared to eat.
Arlene runs the kitchen; she has a repertoire of eggs.
At weekends we get vanilla-speckled crêpes with brown
patches the size of clown mouths. She thinks we need her.
'Haven't I loved you with every force?' she shouts if I say
his name. She'll go up in flames and you can't get near her.
But sometimes something clangs open and I can't help myself,
I'll remember how we lay in bed as the wonky blinds
delivered light. I'm the oldest so I've been out in the world.
I told my sisters. I've seen other ways of doing things.
Heaven help those girls, Arlene says, if they take my broken
spirit for a role model. As if heaven would ever get any

3

kind of look in. We're faraway now. The house is smaller than the light in Arlene's eye. We rock, knees to chest, and put ourselves to bed. We don't know what we'd do without her.

from *The Rialto*

Bird

◊   ◊   ◊

When I became a bird, Lord, nothing could not stop me.

        The air feathered
                        as I knelt
by my open window for the charm –
                        black on gold,
                last star of the dawn.

Singing, they came:
                        throstles, jenny wrens,
jack squalors swinging their anchors through the clouds.

        My heart beat like a wing.

I shed my nightdress to the drowning arms of the dark,
my shoes to the sun's widening mouth.

                Bared,
    I found my bones hollowing to slender pipes,
        my shoulder blades tufting down.
            I   spread   my flight-greedy arms
to watch my fingers jewelling like ten hummingbirds,
my feet callousing to knuckly claws.
            As my lips calcified to a hooked kiss

silence

                then an exultation of larks filled the clouds
and, in my mother's voice, chorused:
        Tek flight, chick, goo far fer the Winter.

So I left girlhood behind me like a blue egg
                                        and stepped off
                        from the window ledge.

How light I was

as they lifted me up from Wren's Nest
bore me over the edgelands of concrete and coal.

I saw my grandmother waving up from her fode,
                    looped
        the infant school and factory,
                        let the zephyrs carry me   out to the coast.

Lunars I flew

                battered and tuneless

        the storms turned me insideout like a fury,
there wasn't one small part of my body didn't blart.

Until I felt it at last   the rush of squall thrilling my wing
                and I knew my voice
was no longer words but song   black upon black.

I raised my throat to the wind
                                and this is what I sang . . .

                    from *Poetry London*

Black Country/Standard
charm/birdsong or dawn chorus   *throstle*/thrush
jack squalor/ swallow   *fode*/yard   *blart*/cry

The Spirit of Geometry

after Magritte

◊　◊　◊

September breeze sorting through the rack of empty swings, a row of absences
easing toward what will never be complete stillness.

The long chains creak – high-pitched, neurotic rigging – the rubber seats still glossed
with this morning's rain. I try to read, leave my children to rebuild their insane estate

and set their incomprehensible laws, a peripheral blur of sandpit, zip-wire, day-glow
dodecahedron, but the text before me merges to a brindled fur where this one stirs

my curiosity – the sagging riddle of damp curls all but covering his eyes; boot-cut
corduroys and a frayed denim jacket buttoned up to the throat. I envy him

his energy, his style, the fact he is so young, the way his face calmly burns with
unspent passion, how he reaches down without complaint, and lifts his son,

who waits with arms raised. They wear more or less identical clothes, the same head
of curly hair – dirty blond in the child's case, darkening to what will certainly become

his father's dirty brown. The boy puts his arms around his father's neck and draws
himself in, and for a split second I convince myself I cannot tell the difference

between the two, see the gargantuan son lift and hold close his tiny father,
the tiny father press his face into the shoulder of his son.

from *Magma*

JAMES BROOKES

Amen to Artillery

for Allen Peterson

◊   ◊   ◊

This American English dictionary
is at its best
in the volume which contains the word 'American'.
So when I talk about Abraham's knife
at Isaac's throat,

I don't just mean *antinomy*
as Kierkegaard might
(the wrongness of a thing which is nonetheless right)
but also the trace metal *antimony*,
that silver, that bone

which is in the steel of the knife to steady it.

from *The White Review*

SAM BUCHAN-WATTS

Nose to Tail

◇　◇　◇

in places far from here, and colder
– like the northern US states Wisconsin, or Alaska –
pigs can freeze to the sides of trucks or have
their limbs crushed by other pigs' limbs

At a gridlock somewhere in North Norfolk
a two-tier truck of livestock waits next to a school bus.
The spotted pigs in the upper tier could be oinking
the most enormous racket, but the bus is icy private
like a cool-box, and from the top deck all you can do
is glance through the slit where the angle makes
the dark pale and mottled rug of upright pigs
inside have no apparent end. In fact,
it is quite difficult to know exactly where one pig stops
and another begins, and the shape of other pigs
in the lattice of pink flesh
make each individual pig's expression seem a smirk
at being privy to this sequestered mass,
chuffed with the pure occasion of it.

from *Clinic*

Supper

◊ ◊ ◊

The Ranunculi, balled-up
little bitches of tissue,

look down their noses,
petals hanging in jowls

while gnarled stems relieve
themselves in the vase.

You fry the food, you add
butter as though you were thin.

An overweight twig
scrapes the window

and says he too would
like to have some butter.

I let him in, and applaud
myself for generosity of spirit

though I make no sound,
fat hands clapping like balloons.

from *Lighthouse*

realspace

◊   ◊   ◊

this is the time and the place of the crash

and who'd have thought when it happened

you'd be sewn up in bed not crying in a stranger's

suit pocket not running out a large building

thinking this building will collapse this

building has already collapsed i've

left my running gear inside not

wishing this was an airplane

disaster with no impending

island paradise not wondering

why people still have train wrecks

not finding yourself on top of an

iceberg that's actually a boat and

the boat is sinking and you're

thinking there's an airlock

labyrinth here and a

small child inside

i've done this

before somewhere

i've rescued her i know

from *Clinic*

At the Entering of the New Year

(Homage to Thomas Hardy)

◇ ◇ ◇

The future isn't what it used to be
YOGI BERRA

Since it's not what it used to be,
the future is ours,

years to regret the bodies we dissolved
in Pinot Noir

and Paracetamol,
a decade or more to walk home in the rain

repeatedly, the yard light coming on
as if by magic;

and, having come this far,
can we take it as read

that nothing ever happens
for a reason,

that choosing is out of the question, as is luck,
and the surest mistake

is to think we already know
what matters when we see it?

A week of fog;
a strange car in the driveway;

a doll's house
in a front yard,

pearled with rain –
no one can read the signs, it's not

a narrative;
if moths know anything of love

it has nothing to do with the beautiful doom
we long for;

and if what we insist on calling
fate seems inexplicable or cruel

it's only because
we lack the imagination

to wish for what it brings,
to brighten it

with something more inventive
than dismay.

Late in the day,
but we're starting to like ourselves

and something feels true
that was always

in doubt
when it counted,

not what we know, but the things
we've decided to keep,

a ribbon of wilderness
out on the rim of our days,

the fine-grain of happy, the snowstorms,
the art of fugue,

some thirteen-minute loop
of grainy footage

running, for auld lang's syne,
at the back of our minds.

from *Times Literary Supplement*

My Beloved

◇   ◇   ◇

Madame, we will meet upon the boulevard,
alternatives being absurd,
some tree-shaded, dust-stippled kerb in the reign of – Napoleon III? –
horse-drawn carriages speed-striped
and blurred as our backdrop. The boulevard itself getting laid.
The fraudulent flounce of your bustle will have me hard,
the severe cut of these breeches, starched
and staid, will not impede my opprobrium. *Merde!*

O Eiffel, your erection casts a long shade.
Your beauty reflects in the gloss of these arcades,
the Benjamin-sprig at your bosom, a disrobing pomade.

You are pregnant, pregnant with the unsaid,
as I am Madame, knowing from either side of this kerb, the boulevard
itself is our true beloved.

from *The Echo Room*

NIALL CAMPBELL

On Eriskay

◊ ◊ ◊

She met me at the fence. A kelpie
who'd stayed too long in this horse form,
she mouthed the sugar on my palm,
and when I slapped her barrel flank
the goose-moor stiffened with a sea
perfume. Gulls gathered on the stoop.

What a way to be seen out: confused
among the pearlwort and the fallow.
Her beach songs, like the recalled taste
of bucket milk, inched from her tongue.
Dusk grew behind the house. I watched
her drink the moon from a moon-filled trough.

from *Granta*

Six Winters

◊ ◊ ◊

1

The fridge has been emptied out
       then filled with snow
and glass milk bottles. Servant bells

       are trembling with your likeness:
                  coy Trachomatis,
   to the sightless
we used to think that everything was black,
             but now we know

       everything is white.
                       A bus shelter.
A bed. The day room at the clinic.

Hail sounding on the roof – white as the eye
   can see. Milk must be skimmed
          before it can be frozen; cultures

   come into being overnight.
             Speech as snowfall,
         sound as prism,
                    vibration as light.

2

The samples in the jars' refrigerated rows,
     secular, invoke you

    who are nowhere to be found,
       who are everywhere. Guardsmen
roll their dice, and from this icy winter

   many families will rise childless.
        The girl in the bleached photograph
still offers up frozen bluebells
       to the camera lens.

But she is grown now, and has learned to live
 with hope. She presses bottles full with snow.
    The couple waits.

Five years. She is deaf to all uncertainty.
Deaf to doctors' superstition;
      to cautious minds.

   Dumb, she sits astride him, her hands
     red with cold.
  Silent, she packs snow in fists
    into his mouth.

3

  Her blindness never stood between her
and the world.
       All sounds occupy
  the place of her closed eyes;
or the smell of incense is rough and dry
under her fingers.
      But the servant bells chime

and you fill her blood. Silently the doors close
    in the gallery:

  the clamour of the portrait hall
a bedchamber now; the dressing table,

wash–stand, chair. Shutters closed
over the blank, whitewashed walls.

Throughout the day
her hands move across the furniture
and with unchanging evening
the child in fretful form.

For a child cannot tell
mistrust from night-time,
forgiveness from return, sleep

from non-existence. Beneath the mist,
the frost is growing deeper;
and what is one more child's life to you?

4

Hope, like all whose hands cradle
a hard-won crown, you understand.
Uncertainty, frenzy, belief
come in sequences of black and thick,

sickening gold. The fridge is packed
with feathers, and row on row of chickens' eggs:

the lamp can barely penetrate
their breathing skins. The noise
of possibility is overwhelming. Not enough

that he should run the pooling yolk
from his hands into hers, hold her body,
pray the rains will come this year.
You,
cockerel-god,
will peck the grain out from the chaff.

You will take the gold straight from the purse.

5

It is the beginning, and music is playing quietly
    under the microscope. As in a dream,
  she can taste it

    the combing of hair, the static of jumpers,
  the threading of glove to red woollen glove.

    New colours arise from milk spilt on paper,
or hands press out lions
        from pink plasticine:
       a nerve cell will die
  every time she imagines
  (each time sudden drowning)
  how it will be. Meadowsweet, soil,

  saliva, urine, blood droplets idling
    in ambering wine.
       Stoppered,
each neck holds a feather of eider.
    Each neck holds the white noise
  of caught butterflies.

6

Lend her her eyes, and if she is sightless
  she will touch closed eyelids
  and with fingertips
      trace the globes below.

Lend her her body, here in the waiting room
where all eyes are upon her but hers.
     Has she everything she needs,

the shape of her estate, the full enclosure
    of each breath? What can she call her own?
Two hearts, two bodies: only she
    can sense the boundaries within,

  hidden from our sight. There is sleet
  brushing the window. Daytime TV. The clattering

of a backbone of coloured wooden beads
and the shriek of a young girl. All is calm

in her map of ragged breaths, clutched hands
and magazines; and you are nowhere
to be seen.

from *Poetry London*

The Daffodil

◊   ◊   ◊

Little son, you've spun that daffodil out
Onto the waves to the sea, onto the melting edge
Of continuousness it floats. Its lostness terrifies you.
Your curls sing in the wind like a daffodil's flute.

There's so much in that single act of surrender.
What did you mean – you, who's more flower than man?
Oblation? To put to death? Or just to see its glamour
Against the waves? O, the sea is in multiples; it blurs

At your feet. In your mind, there are no replicas.
All of the world appears of a piece. Did you think
The sea might put forth buds and turn to spring?
Not a chance. Its greys are jingling with old wars.

In time, you'll have a recurring dream of a car that takes
You away from me. The lostness of the daffodil will grow
In you again. Out there, in the grey, each golden cell
A synecdoche of what you once held, once threw.

from *Poetry London*

from *calling a spade a spade*

◊ ◊ ◊

The N Word

You came back as rubber lips, pepper grains, blik
you're so black you're blik and how the word stuck to
our tongues eclipsing – or so we thought – the fear
that any moment anyone might notice
and we'd be deemed the wrong side of a night sky.
Lately you are a *pretty little lighty* who can
get dark because – even now – dark means street
which means beast which means leave now for Benfleet.
These days I can't watch a music video
online without you trolling in the comments
dressed to kill in your new age binary clothes.

from *Poetry Review*

Figtree

◊   ◊   ◊

He trepans with the blunt
screwdriver on his penknife:
unripe figs require the touch
of air on flesh to sweeten.
Blind, but in his fingertips
he has the whole knot
of this figtree memorised.

The five inch scar, a vague
felt mesh of parallelogram,
was where he bandaged up
a split branch once.
He starts from there,
first handheight fruit
and then he gets the ladder.

Gauge weight, turn, unturn.
He sings beneath his breath
about the excellence of figs,
their mellowness,
their skin–dints
like the perfect undulation
in the small of his wife's back.

from *The White Review*

DAVID CONSTANTINE

Foxes, rain

◊　◊　◊

Waking I heard the foxes in next door's garden.
They have eviscerated a black bag.
They are hungry, they want to live as long as possible.
And I dozed, woke again, heard only the rain
And could not imagine it other than black
Falling hard, a copious black rain. I hope my friend
Is not lying sleepless tonight. He has no appetite,
He has pain, he lies during daylight in the living room
Under a blanket by the fire and can't get warm.
Daylight today will crawl out nearly dead
From under an inexhaustible cold rain.
My neighbour parting his curtains will be sickened
How much there was to eat still in his guts.

from *Poetry London*

Some Curious Thing II

◊ ◊ ◊

Present Synchronicity

so not to choose the wrong afterimage narrative past gets removed from
this place that's as real / fake as anything else

each sign replaced by a form, each form transcribed to an act. We wear
our acts differently as moods. It turns out baby never even *knew*

how to interpret the difference between you & your life

how to see error dangling

that's keen on Conscience & a certain Concept of Duty too

★

just as a bird the only bird to fly backwards landing aloft means death or
surprise at the watering hole. We know what we are but not what, etc.

the prize goes to s/he who can beat the air with its wings long enough
to deflect the sun's rays from my eyes – given yr precursor in the shape
of gold, and already exist for that. On the other hand. Profanity violence
irony grace of Sunday all that

(god as Light/er than feather/plant/animal)

& but over the years science has proved light enters the eye the same as desire enters the will to believe in science: a pinprick, a hole of desire – black & white era of common sense (fetish)

how we negotiate this mystery isn't scatter your love in the clouds like mirrors, pour rich filings in the sea below

or religion in the Form of Art

★

so maybe it is about sewing the will through the hole till it exists or is melted or on the third axis (of imaginary numbers only). Counting your assets daily won't save others from the

quiet little engine, she's so wanted to be loved, she doesn't want to be loved. I.e., always the indeterminate unknown term to be sung after!

& although but in the extreme point of mathematical (difference) the curve is really a plane on a grid, two things that add up to this dual meaning of mind *and spirit*. Living extremely daily. What's not to love about such ambivalence

Euridice enters the tunnel of faith & our tongues our minds turn to the stupidity of dust our dwellings are flooded, our forests, fire – naturally – this could have been represented another way

more than each personal show of worth

memory scene darted afterwards under cover of being 'helpful'. Its reel unfolding night after night after night after night after night after night after night after night after night

just in case you tried any sudden moves

*

Still Life

so that closer & closer, & backwrds & backwards, we come to the point: there is always this something not quite ticked off the flow chart, not dyed fully under the seeing scope. How beautifully epistemic, how it robs us of hope & despair, prompts us to dive & fly this petite object

still we go to the movies, attend. In the cinema's headlights it puts on grey lipstick and swoons for a lover. Only afterwards do we learn this is not real life

expect some god to rush in, save the story where angels have left

& this not quite object (so petite you mayn't even have missed it) – the why humans differ, the ex out of naught. or one is more violent, one works till its fingers form tiny fins, or turns its guns till they pop like a cartoon war. Wait, that's not right

how we are gather stories unto ourselves, little appendages, that work necessary under water

or how those who believe in the Death of Mystery hope more than others

★

meantime the optics of nerves are all pointed skyward (to money & objects), but under the little scope, a not insignificant sample really does feel (once it gets the impression of being looked at). Surprising how, having passed over that once, gives such large amounts back: causing internal glow brightness. Sudden Spike in the Trend

& it's too too silly to think how we might live differently if our scope were different: more love tenderness comically tragically whatever. On the scale of justice (1 to 10) we get what's due to a logic of passing, but old as the dust that crawled out the desert floor. Though he might wish enslavement, might even crawl to that object of love, the horizon is always de facto at the end of the line one never reaches. A fish hook, its mouth dangling. Desert-ridiculous. *Unterwegs* language

never ask me about that OK ask me about that

★

start with the fatality of the intellectual partitions of the Universe (into exactly two: a & not-a) that causes joint exhaustion, not to say mutual suspicion. Correlates of the law of identity which is the first principle of feeling-thought. Or may be the weaker term of the equation (thought-laughter)? For our 'ordinary knowing' has before itself only the object – & how she is passing fair, but lets the ball slip out of his hands. Rolls down stairs – just out of touch

so that closer & closer,
& away & away

& trash is made up to look precious & furniture suddenly swells to inor-
dinate size. Our perceptions have got to be fucked, else we are regressing
again

*

experience which is much too obvious & not enough to warn one of the
same extant whole – which is the reason for the act of knowing & not the
object alone. But also the ego that knows, and the relation of I to object
to another, i.e. consciously

but what simple pleasure to dissolve into fire's mouth though stupid you
know how it burns, better swallow you up & change there where you
just couldn't stand it you loved it you lay helping yourself to the pips as
well as the juice

although in common likewise to things. In (other) words: they as not taken as is but rather in definite waves of who they are. Human condition of unfortunate prevalence. We could turn our attention to dying yellow animals – but is it all one? So all we can do is that

write all the things you see in a summer scape note that down: all flora & fauna. Now do not experience joy till you have collected those numbered & organised prodded & lied to, maybe mistaken for some female sample # bla

do you want to say something do something write something go after all that was left before she in all her unique commonness leaves your view-finder for ever that one day

★

Coming To Presently

another way to say that might be in numbers or song – if only those things had not meant to be funny but actually real. & former ways of seeing called 'Realism,' better, 'Idealism.' Here are to be considered the general determinations of things. This is no conjecture, not even a cantata, though delivery of it may be a little piano piano or nothing at all. Look!

the subject, more definitely seized, is that (golden) apple – the sensuous glinting, foregrounded aura – you no longer want it as much. Understanding (the object) now has this character. It is pure accident, also an abidingly (soft) side. Gets softer with air til it's suddenly coming apart in yr hands & we throw that back what else could we do

but she too looked back it was not all to blame (him). There isn't a question in space where innocence isn't partly a blank apple, partly an open face. Irreducible equation: epiphany (of the coin dropping slowly as well)

★

& the extent to which SPACE is constructed is an interesting question it is always an interesting question to write back the projection of body or SPACE or urban creatures, who look suddenly cute snuffling round in the trash, but then go for a baby's face thinking it to be a perfectly innocent apple. This in turn sets that, like a fugue or a serious question framed partly in London against a backdrop of fire or crime, partly somewhere else altogether

or just invest it with the ability to look at us back

(& we meant to crawl but my heels got stuck in this rigid paradigm, just like the love got caught in my hair)

now specifically suddenly lights a period of time (which will be seen in the dim light of future arrangements) – not only in green, if you are thinking that dumb, but also its compliment red which will make it vibrate. Or corrupt it to worldliness.

& how not to do otherwise?

from *Poetry Wales*

Trompe l'oeil

◊ ◊ ◊

The night of research
is over. The ideas have come.
We are judged by an old suit.
The small light on his microphone burns red.

I want to float out,
escape up through that Baroque vault
past stone ramparts into blue
welcome of angels. A woman presses

her idea against
the mahogany barrier
kneading at the sculpted wood.
When she lies down idea-less later

I would lie in her
arms for ever if that would help her sleep.

from *Shearsman*

Ode to a 1980s Baton Twirling World Champion

◇ ◇ ◇

The baton rolls and blurs asp-like around
girl neck. O elastic Cleopatra
Amphetamina, stung insanity,
hounded by a sound like a bumblebee.

O pink puck, you buck, hurl; maenad Odette
whirling out the jewel box. Frou-frou roulette,
tricking probability. O rah-rah'd
neon imp, you out-fox flexible bounds,

tempestuous flea, fugitive judo,
impeccable feat. In the final beats,
you flourish like a grinning flamingo,
big eyes to the bleachers, big empty seats.

from *3:AM Magazine*

Babysitting in the Crematorium

Translated by Elin ap Hywel

◊   ◊   ◊

Such a strange place to be, little one,
a parked car on a Friday afternoon
in January, you and I claiming

this hour for ourselves. We have
a world full of fancies between our fingers,
each rattle-shake a shock,

till the sound brings a smile. And beyond us
is grief's aisle, a grave company
witness to the loved one, resting in peace.

Unlike us, then. We are unwounded,
but bound together with a sling, near
an endless earth-bank. See, how easily

the moles do it. Sweet hillocks
hillfort the earth. Parties in soil,
in sheer delight of their hidden lives,

these recyclers of air delving deeper and deeper,
digging on down to the bottom of things,
drawing out each life, rebreathing each breath.

Humanity does not have this gift.
Beauty for ashes is what brings us
to this hot spot. We were born for the smoke.

But for now, my little one, sleep gently.
How eternal each second when minding a child.
And our lives from now on? Quakegrass, lightning.

Carco yn y Crem

◇ ◇ ◇

Fy mechan, lle rhyfedd i fod
ar b'nawn Gwener yn Ionawr –
mewn cerbyd stond gan haeru'r

awr inni ein hunain. Byd
llawn dychmygion sy rhwng ein dwylo,
pob rhuglyn yn syn o'i siglo

nes troi'r sain yn wên. Y tu draw in
mae eil i alar, mintai ddwys
yn dystion i un sy'n gorffwys.

Nid fel nyni. Dianafus ydym,
wedi ein rhwymo â gwregys, ger clawdd
nad oes terfyn iddi. Sbia, mor hawdd

yw ffordd gwahaddod. Twmpathau glân
yn gorseddu'r pridd. Partïon o bridd,
yn dathlu'n foddhaus eu heinioes gudd

y rhai sy'n twrio'n is ac yn is, lawr
i'r dyfnder pell wrth ail-fyw eu hanadl,
ailgylchwyr aer yn estyn pob hoedl.

Y rhin hon, nid yw'n eiddo i'r ddynolryw.
Harddwch at lwch yw'r hyn a'n dwg
i'r fangre boeth. Fe'n magwyd i'r mwg.

Ond yr awr hon, cwsg yn esmwyth fy 'mach i.
Mor dragwyddol yw ennyd o warchod plentyn.
Hyn dry weddill ein dyddiau yn fellt ar laswelltyn.

from *Mslexia*

39

MacNeice's Mother

◇   ◇   ◇

MacNeice's mother wore a yellow dress.
It was a daffodil and candle-flame.
A moon for moths that lit the nursery's darkness.
And when he called out in the night, one came.
And when he cried out in darkness one was there
or when there was a pain. This call and answer,
– need being met, some longing stopped with care –
became a single thing, as when together
two muscles pulled together on the bone
to move a limb – or rowers who, mid-stream,
forgot the separate parts that each one played . . .
That is say that he was not alone
when in the darkness, in a kind of dream
they talked as one: the unborn and the dead.

from *Poetry London*

avoid using the word 'pussy'

◊ ◊ ◊

feminists it's time to become angry
again! gingerbread women break your
fists when they say

the punk rock girl band / stop bitching
whose name we can't say / i call them bitches
on morning television / because they are bitches

three strumpets who will / holy mary mother of god
be pardoned soon

the girls are sinners, they've made their
choice against christ & real madonna
what pussies, when riots?

but which of you weren't always angry –
who listened / stop bitching
little heart elbow patches

are used only because
they're hard to take seriously.
everyone can be pussy riot?

but why presume / stop bitching

but the struggle as its own apart
but the struggles together.

the trampled tents laughing
i hate i despise / the empty church
& do not respect

your festivals / what if we had two
hundred thousand years more of this

& if you are not angry from before
these times / what riots

will you have had enough / stop
will you stop? pussy like most slang terms
(see also: cunt) an endearing name

for a girl / do not endear
when riots are / which anger is this

from *Clinic*

Seven Rounds with Bill's Ghost

◊　◊　◊

Those who remember you
as gentle, a point-scorer –
well, they remember you,
I'll give them that.
Oh aye, mild as the wet
of a cat's nose – with a lick
like the rough of its tongue.
Before you got that dicky lung
you could be found, I hear,
exhaling soft advice
through the cherry on your fag.

Propped against the headgear,
I expect, disinclined
to swear or nip behind
for a piss. A good sport, though,
Aye, always laughing
was Bill. Pint-size but useful
in the ring. St John's Ambulance man.
I often think of you as I can:
scarecrowed in an album,
improving, tough to digest,
a bit like bran. Sweeter, mind,

and sometimes linen-shirted,
tanning at a furious rate
in Bournemouth, always with
your son and a vanilla cone,
that grin like a smashed accordion.
Or, much later, convulsed
at every gag in Disney's *Robin Hood*,
oodelallying, while the same son stood

wondering about the time
and if my nappy needed changing
as we both gurgled on the sofa.

Those who remember you,
they've not been backward
in coming forward. Still waxing
about your weave and bob,
your pathological manias
for fair play. So I wonder:
say some chancer pulled a stunt
and it rubbed you wrong – say just the once –
would you ever drop the pipsqueak act
and show him? Say this bloke
might give his wife a little tap.

No sterner lessons
for him, no sneaky
dab of side? I hear you
have to come down hard
and with a twist. Imagine
the parabola, the swoop,
the dash of cranberry as he hits the deck,
the look on the cunt as you wring his neck
and give him something
to slap about. Christian
justice, we could call it.

No, just the lenient jog
to deacon duty, boxing clever,
and clever you were, *Aye,*
never stretched, past the advent
of Tommy Cooper, to the first
and final trip abroad,
when the kinking light on Lake Geneva
dazzled you into a seizure –
did you not laugh then,
like a creaking outhouse loo?
Or when that last stroke mullered you.

But, Bill, listen,
I'm on Chippy Lane
at chuck-out, and it's all turned
to a gully of garlic sauce.

44

We've a lad by the smut shop
giving it 'Darling' this
and 'Blue Army' that – some skin slinging
shawarma too close to that poor sod ringing
his girl from a doorway –
and he might be in want
of a word.

from *Poetry Wales*

MATTHEW GREGORY

A Room in Taiwan, 2010

◊   ◊   ◊

And how many desert miles of the web
has she crossed tonight searching
for the home address of Mastroianni.

Mastroianni is no longer among us.
She doesn't know this so continues
her drift from one ruined domain

to the next one, signing herself in
to empty guestbooks as she goes.
I would like to write to Mr Marcello Mastroianni

please if anyone know where he is.
I dream us in light of stars and great city Rome.
I want to be like kiss of Anita Ekberg.

Mastroianni whose thousand pictures
in these forums lose him on pages
like palimpsests of man on top of man

where this girl, at her tropical desk,
who lists for his deep, romantic heart
touches a hit-counter, once, in the dark.

from *Poetry Review*

PHILIP GROSS

The Works

(for Katy Giebenhain and Stephanie Gibson)

◇   ◇   ◇

. . . and what did the store room contain
once it was empty?
                        Beyond dust,

something scorched, a tyre-burn, half metallic,
on the smell-horizon; and

the silence of downed tools – be exact:
that of particular names
                        (gear hobber,

core or ribbon blender), true names
someone would have known

as if by nature *(pre-cured tread press, cold
feed extruder)*
                    like the snug in the palm

of a lever or grip, *(dispersal kneader,
pelletiser)* metal warming to the hand

that used it. No generic silence, this,
but particular gaps
                      in the air, the way

the absences of *hardy, top fuller, slack
tub* linger in specific corners

of a converted smithy, or this and that

47

endearment
                    (add your own

here if you have them) in the language
of a worn out love.

                    from *Magma*

DAVID HARSENT

Effaced

◊　◊　◊

A life beyond the life and known to no one, peopled by ghosts
who can step up to be fleshed if you choose, or be held back,

can be dreamwork, can walk straight in, the invited guests
you welcome and fear. You speak for them, you give them what they lack,

you note what can't be said, you feel them out, keep track
of their night-lives, night-moves, hallways, hidden rooms,

all of which delights you, moving among them, shrouded in black,
widowed without being wed, feeding the fire, if you want to, with reams

of work half-done and left to grow in silence, that precious stack
curling and catching – last love, last light – as you burn whatever rhymes.

from *Poem*

STUART HENSON

The Builder

(after the prose-poem 'Le Maçon' by Aloysius Bertrand)

◊   ◊   ◊

Way up there where he's treading the scaffolded air, drill in
hand, a spirit of the great gold dome's reflections, Ahmed Nasib
stands astride with his feet on a skyline of block-work and spires,
its thirty sharp minarets – the horizon's finials.

He's singing along to a song in his ear while the adhan flares
from the mouths of the tower to the street-void below, to the
cliff falls of concrete and glass and the shell-gape that nestles the
slant of a kestrel's motionless wing . . .

While he watches the fort, with its pastry-cut walls crimped like
a star; the compound; the hospital; the checkpoint . . . And even
so distant the guards with their helmets, their lip-mics and aerials,
the bulk of their blast-flaps, their body armour.

In sunlight the screen of a humvee winks back, and slowly the
shadows are turning about the mast on the landing-strip and the
look-out post and the squat white bricks of the peace-keepers'
four-by-fours.

And there's more: in the stadium where the dust whips up into
miniature ghosts that hurry a moment then stumble, exhale,
Ahmed Nasib observes through the heat the police popping a
shy of tin cans from one pockmarked crossbar.

Till at last in the dusk when the broad mosaic floor of the
mosque is rolled up into shade, he looks out from his ladder
across to the village far off – a comet against the blue of the night
where the houses are burning, the rockets still fall.

from *Modern Poetry in Translation*

Poem in Which

◇ ◇ ◇

She always leaves
a bacon sandwich on the kitchen table,
a message scribed in ketchup beneath its upper rung of bread.
In which I swallow whole the note and never know it's there.
I spell I'm sorry with sodden clothes, with smiling too long and flower stems,
on my mistakes, as they are happening, all of them.
Poem in which my mother is maddened, not disappointed.

Poem in which all my mothers are maddened: the old ladies
smoking at bus stops, scanning bacon and bread loaves at Tesco,
under flapping umbrellas in King's Cross and High Barnet. Poem in which
I forget my umbrella, am not a failure and my mothers,
all of them, are pretty and called Margaret.
        In which the rain spells their name on me
and dry patches of escarpment.

from *Poem in Which*

Scrying: turpentine

◇　◇　◇

The rack dislimns, and makes it indistinct,
As water is in water
　　　　　　　　— *Antony and Cleopatra*, 4.14

When the last turps-
dipped filbert has stirred
its tinkling storm —

damp hair tendrilled
at the neck as silk
that leaps as it burns
or the swallow weaves
its nest of heaven-
fretted auguries &
the snuffed taper lifts
its last dragonish
gasp tonguing as that
first forked squall
of milk in tea or how
panic's cascade flips
one bloomed neuron
to a lit-up city madder
& alizarin fugitive
pigments phantasms
tamed at last as every-
thing is to vesper's
tincted murk & think
without this primordial
pool our irised eye
can never clasp itself
frail apple & the sky

shrinks to a jamjar
a glassful of trickling
earth where light
parts from dark &
water from water

– a day's rest delivers
an inch of purest liquor;
soul after sin.

    from *PN Review*

from *Natural History*

◇   ◇   ◇

Of Elephants

The clemancie of Elephants. How elephants
breed and how they disagree with Dragons.

How they make sport in a kind of Morrish dance.
The elephant who wrote Greeke and read musicke.

The elephant who cast a fancie and was enamoured upon
a wench in Egypt who sold nosegaies and wickerishe.

Their hornes, or properly Teeth, of which men make
images of the gods, fine combes, wanton toies.

Who march alwaies in troupes. Who snuffe and puffe.
Who the troublesome flie haunts.

Who cannot abide a rat or a mouse. Who are purified
by dashing and sprinkling themselves with water.

Who, enfeebled by sicknesse, lie upon their backes,
casting and flinging herbs up toward heaven.

Who adore and salute in their rude manner that planet,
the moone.

from *Poetry Review*

What I'll Say When I Get Back

◇ ◇ ◇

This is the place, I'll say, no one and nothing
but a two-seat bench I'll sit on by myself
(because I will have come alone) and only the sound
of the river (which could be the Aire) behind my back,
the fields folding out to something like a town
beyond, and there's the path that brought me here
replete with dog turd and sheep shit and rocks
and puddles and muck which will take me back,
if I like, under the streetlights which won't yet be lit,
past the manicurist and used-car garage,
and then the all familiar turn-in to my avenue,
to my back door, the empty wine and beer bottles
I must get round to recycling, missed calls
I should return. But if I'll hold on
I'll see the path goes on and is the path
I might yet take, leading as it does
past the last pylons and last of the kept horses,
to more of the sound of more of the river.

from *Edinburgh Review*

Sea-Music

◇   ◇   ◇

In one of the forgotten places of the earth,
The end of the Hammersmith and City Line
On a little island made from builders' waste,

Stands a single palm, patched and peeling, tattered
Tropical bird – *its fire-fangled feathers*
Dangle down . . . As I walk past it to the 8:09

I can hear palms rustle in the tropic airs,
I can hear sea-music, sirens singing,
Snatches of gentle ukulele songs,

The small waves' whisper of *shush, shush*;
I can taste the *tristesse* of a tropical berth,
A warm wind from the barrier-reef bringing

Sticky-sweet of rum, salt of panties and thongs
Those wriggling sirens yanked down in their haste,
The salt-sweetness that is uniquely theirs;

I can see the tattoos – a tiny patch of home,
The shadow-island, parakeet and palm,
Just below the panty-line, above the bush;

Can see the moon through shutters stripe an arm,
Outflung, a flattened breast – the fleck of foam,
The just-fucked look in grey-green eyes, like sea-mist! . . .

A sea wind shakes the palms and rocks the sea-bed
And a faint glow dancing in the fine salt spray
Leads me where I'm led. *This*, the sirens say,

Was not your true course; why did you steer it?
Because to you all places were the same?
Infernal joys, joys of the deadened spirit.

You went to where a tree stood like a flame
That flickered in the petrol-glare; you learnt to fear it.
No place of safety and no berth free from blame.

Infernal joys of night-time, deadened spirit
On your tongue, your tongue hot as a flame
And the insects uttering their prayer. Who would hear it?

You looked for comfort but no comfort came
On the tundra's permafrost. Your deadened spirit
Flickered in the glare of its own shame.

Look. The compass, shattered. You daren't go near it.
Now everyone is dead, all places are the same.
You looked for comfort but no comfort came.

Then they are gone to spindrift, lost in air . . .
It seems I know this place, each creek and cove
Though when I saw it last, I can't remember:

A wide expanse, flat as the sands at Camber,
Cloud-hung, all paths leading to a concrete pillbox –
Piss-smelling floor, condoms like the ghosts of cocks,

Dried seaweed and turds – not the promised home
Or place of safety! – and a glint like amethyst
In violet eyes – that dutiful daughter . . .

Could this be where she's decided it must end? –
Not in some hotel bar, black velvet skirt
And pearls, her ash-blond hair cut shorter –

The way I've seen her look up from her glass of wine
And say, 'So you've finally found me, as if I were
A broken toy you'd thrown away and picked up again,

Wondering how much it might cost to mend . . .
So much pain, so much you're prepared to deny –
What is it, bygones bygones, that old line?

57

Or are you wondering if I can still be had
For the price of a double at the Grand –
Are you sick or mad? Don't you understand

How much I wanted you, how much it hurt?
How I used to pray you'd come back, or else die
Calling out for me . . . ?' Instead I hear these words,

You will always belong here, no matter where you rove.
Your 'poetry' – still want to be the Baudelaire
De nos jours, or a cut-price Byron, mad, bad

And dangerous? I don't see much mileage in it –
Your youth is gone, you're getting older by the minute.
The thought of what's to come leaves you shit-scared.

Once it would have been the syphilis that got you,
Or opium, or drink – things that would rot you
From the inside out; or a husband would have shot you . . .

Bid farewell to shipmates who are gone, while you've been spared –
But not for long – and set sail, for those fortunate isles
Where the only commuting is in nautical miles,

Where the men are men and the women are all smiles;
They lie about you, your errors and your wrecks,
One course left open. Set sail. Clear the decks.

from *New Walk*

CHRIS McCABE

The Alchemist

◊ ◊ ◊

Spoken by Lovewit who returns to the London he fled to
escape the plague to find his home overrun with the ruses
and deceptions of conmen Face, Subtle and Dol Common.
Face wins a reprieve by stage-managing Lovewit's marriaqe
with the woman he has fallen in love with, Dame Pliant. We
are here, Blackfriars, 1610.

Will you be my speculatrix?   absence keeps us
guessing   this city can lick figs, I'll gum its silks
with cláy   *stuck full of black & melancholic worms*
     The old St Pauls was búrnt of trade & commerce
this hollow dóme's for confessions   blue was the life
motif for summer   & the youth you saw in my face
     London expells me twice weekly with plágue   the
provinces re-hearse my art   like a coal stuffed with
diamonds the wax splits at Eúston   the zòmbiés of
ambition   march policies of truth   but poets are
liars, the wind whórls their value phones   I'm on
loan with words of àccént rísing   the terraces
I've come from   dictionary entries in duplicates
     definition FIRE licks my heels   Christ's blood in

carafes at business lunches   less toxic than sodium glúta-
mate   income enough to learn German   or go
back to therapy   Hoch Deutsch was not at Bábel   I
consort with the small poets of our time
   the tooth fairy tweaks their nibs each night   and
milk leaks out each morning   When the bawd of
Lambeth meets the bard of Southwark   you get
another fuckin Revenger's play *This night, I'll change all,*
that is metal, in thy house, to gold   even the blàck fillings
in this skull   that are rocks around the skinned seal
of the tongue   if I show them when I laugh
   that's because to laugh is the anti-death
   even against the city's new plágue   named
COMMUTE   There is no travelcard

to takes us back   I have a real toy sword but am in the
wrong play   strung for a woman who circulates like
oil   whórled with rubber & roses
a *bonnibell*, the text said   a soft & buxom widow
to this live skeleton   rattled with libido

from *Poetry Review*

JOHN McCULLOUGH

!

◊   ◊   ◊

It entered creation as sudden as angel
or injury – the stacked letters of *io*, a pillar of fire.
Already it is intimate with bishops, philosophers,
flouting borders, stowed in the peppered tails
of sentences. It infiltrates vaults, prisons,
the bedrooms of kings. I have tried to resist
but it steals from my nib, its saucy eye
rippling in candlelight, dodging pumice
and knife. Mr Smythe disapproves, names it
a feminine indulgence, the want of self-restraint.
Like Lord Allwright's secretary in greeting,
his hand travelling the road of my spine.
That tap on my rear that made verticals
govern my dreams. At night, I see vellum
with one symbol for sheet after sheet,
inscribed in blue light. My ankles vanish
and I exist, suspended, above my rounded feet.
I am always at the end of terraces, waiting
till I'm near him again, recover my form and can say
Here I am – a hot fountain in the garden
of language. The scratch of the vanquished,
those undone by the world, staring back
at the hand that shaped me, astonished.

from *Poetry London*

Doors and Windows of Wallonia

◇ ◇ ◇

Before Television backlit them with its haunted blues,
its gauze of voice over voice, dubbings of *Dynasty* and *Dallas*,
there were firesides filtered through net curtains, shadows
pulling free from shadows. The furniture didn't furnish,
it loomed; heavy as cannon, it boomed darkness.

After closedown, after the trembling not-quite-stasis
of the RTB testcard, the blue glow lingered,
fizzed against mosquito nets, caught the flypaper garlands
with their incrustation of bluebottle and *mouche à merde*,
the banal shitfly with his coalface glitter.

That was the house's pulse, a comatose cellar-beat
to which my grandmother, Bouillon's only dressmaker,
pedalled kilometres of stitching, threaded her needles
seven to seven in daylight that took all day to die.
Her only books were swatches; she held them up

to the daughters and widows of Wallonia
fresh with their ideas from Brussels, of haute couture,
their cut-outs from Paris-Match: a small-town catwalk
of Deneuves along a corridor of Stockman mannequins
stuck with pins, stained with oil or grease, and for me then

(for me still) so oddly sexual with their tapered waists,
the perfection of their closedness. My face at the window,
I'd watch her busy sparrow-jerks inside the darkness that fleshed her out,
and smell the last-but-one all-day *pot-au-feu* that held its own
against the clashing scents of factory-owners' wives.

But the body that stayed caught in the full-length looking-glass
is mine, my drowning childhood pulling down, and these days
nothing – least of all my whole life – flashes by. Only the empty
mirror gives me back that time, and the lace curtains,
more air than lace, are sieves for shadows to pass through light.

Each time I breathe I breathe it in, that sublimate of all that's gone.
Essence of Indoors would be the perfume, if they made it.

from *Literary Review*

EDWARD MACKAY

Afterword

for Tsutomu Yamaguchi

◊   ◊   ◊

Twice licked by lightning, this man like a comet
passes twice across the blank pulse of sky to make

his shadow stand, unhitched from flesh, etched to tarmac
and brickwork in two cities, at once. He cannot make time

stop again, as it did twice, the clocks totemic
with their cracks and twice-right times, unravelling meiotic

new light from the old, a world, twice tipped to dark. Commit
again the crime of chance, slough off, again, all yet to come

or live as stains of carbon, chemical scum, the automatic
offspring of unchoosing chance. So choose. Come to

the edge, again, and leap, again: eyes ablaze, atomic.

from *Shearsman*

ANDREW McMILLAN

if it wasn't for the nights

◊   ◊   ◊

I tour my foreign voice
through the tin roofed halls of semi rural provinces
I barely understand the lines
but the crowd goes mad and claps
of thunder thrum the valley where I sleep
and my lonelyhaircut cellist eyes the bar between us
and I gargle salt   and sleep alone
and back across the border the man I love is curled
to someone else   and they don't speak a word
and   outside   a precious bird doesn't comprehend
the language of its wings
and frost hums on the weathervane

if it wasn't for the nights   Steffan   I'd come home

from *The Rialto*

Mind

◊ ◊ ◊

a shoal's ten-thousands deflected by a threat
to a river of silver burnishing an edge

a carpet of dirty pigeons in a square
bursting like popcorn round a child's hot dash

a living grub, wasp-needled, slung and buried,
hemmed by the ripen of the pending eggs

two plants contesting a nook in rock,
the earnest, slow-grind deathmatch of their roots

a field mouse, mouthing a pup's scruff,
juggling the grass-stalks' seedhead clubs

a weakened hind yet staggering through woods,
pursued by a dog that long since panted home

a carp landed, bucketed, its dumbstruck lips
o'ing for hours and hours and hours

a rutting bison, high on his reek,
crashing, rolling, willing the world's shake

a spider, gossamer, launched and riding
into the future on a silken wish

from *Iota*

Finlandia

◊   ◊   ◊

What I know about death is Sibelius
on the high-fidelity music centre, dad
listening in the dark, gas off, still
in his wind cheater with corduroy trim;
Sibelius so high it distorts the angles of the day;
Sibelius until the street light's eye
is replaced by a cold sun's watch,
by which time my dad has remade my mother
into a living woman, so that we are
not driving the three hundred miles north –
through a slurry of questions with two dogs,
no answers and the wrong clothes for the weather –
just to be with him, and, my sisters similarly,
are not made small again by her absence –
not lost on a day out in Cleethorpes,
waiting at school gates or serving endless
PG Tips and fig biscuits that no one's
going to touch; no, my dad plays Sibelius
with the windows wide, so unfathomably loud
that the neighbours hear it the length of the street;
unaware of this remaking of the day's events
they don't hammer the walls with their shoes
or come to the door to reason or try even
to blot it out with Nat King Cole,
Deanna Durban or Manuel's *Music of the Mountains*,
instead they listen, mourn in their living rooms,
perhaps with a small port or Mackeson's,
so that *Coronation Street, The Bill,*
News at Ten, all have this soundtrack
behind them . . . and across town
in Arthur Gresty's chapel, my mother
might also feel the thud, her blue lips

warming, parting, and for a moment
breathing again; so what I know is the strength
of my mother's love, the volume of my father's.

from *Poetry London*

The Redeemers

◊   ◊   ◊

I danced, with my shirt soaked and bones broken I danced because the pain made me smile. I danced faster, with bruises all over my face, blood everywhere, and I danced the song of no one fucking cares. I danced in the middle of the avenues, looking sick as a dog and, oh sweet jesus, it hurt but I couldn't get enough of it. And I danced back over the road knowing it was killing me, passing by the newsstands, and down the subway stairs into the cave. It was filled with riches, treasures piled on top of the other, with thousands of dead black boys stretched out in the ashes. In the cave there were jewels, black jewels: they just lay there waiting for all the black boys to discover them. I practically fell over them, and I knew I'd never be able to stop now. I danced because the boys were all so fucking beautiful, and because I just wasn't fast enough. I danced the song of no one fucking cares for the thousands of dead black boys that lay dead in the ashes. I danced to them:

The Redeemers

Together with the suns
before them
beneath the amber,

they push their carts
to the midst of the barrens,
to where
the steep roads are met
by dispossession and loss. The hope

is for day, always, the richest binds
they heft to the night
pioneers of the nameless,
bound to the discovered weight
with no tale to sell.
Scribe the sodden bins,

They said it was what desire entails, the blood and the semen and all the little precious things that fade and wane. I had all my belongings with me, and was about to exit the gates, together with my boys behind me, but the fuckers wouldn't let it be. They left me there for hours hanging from my arms – the dumb stupid fucks – waiting for me to make a statement. They took me out to the marshes, and the other bloke, the one with the bad smell, then started in on me. He had a blade in his hand and it made a noise as it went in. He was hardcore. Real cutting edge. I would've danced for him if he'd wanted me to. But I was too shy and frightened, even with the blood whistling in my ears, and

the unwanted.
In the darkened cities
comb through the drifts,
the thinnest shards of plentiful loss.

Scavengers:
make the task take the heart forward,
lest all be lost
to abandon, to a world without hunger or restraint.
Taste it in your mouths
these tithes that prosper, without risk or remembrance:
sacrifices. Beggars of the never was.

Push these carts:
you do not know how far they've come,
you do not know of their return, or belonging,
come,
take up the life-day dirt
on your way to the depots
looking for the signs (the anointing),
but seeing nothing but dust.

the smell of my own shit telling me I
was no longer up for doing any business.
That's how I arrived at the blue cave.
The stupid saga started there. That's
how it began: the love affair that left me
wasted but ever eager to have it all, now,
the stink that reveals the kill.

from *Snow*

Christmas Seven Times Seven

◇ ◇ ◇

Seven-times-seven of these
till now, one spent alone.
I watch first lights come on
on a houseboat by the dim canal.
There are two whole families
somewhere on the earth I'll call
who wouldn't be surprised.

Seven-times-seven of these.
I woke up eye to eye
with my little zombie tree
whose blue-green-crimson bulbs still light
a path through other trees
to the beckoning unearthly spot
if I thin my eyes and think so.

Seven-times-seven. Today
falls on a Saturday,
like a tramp who's trying to say
it's Saturday to the holy beaming
family riding by,
their tinsel tied and fluttering,
their kindness claiming *his* kind

though seven-times-seven times
in fifty times they leave him
wordless by a dustbin.
The early light is pale and tinted,
precious, this one time
I've nothing much to bring it
but our old words for numbers.

Seven-times-seven breaths
and something comes, as if
the dark won't stand for it,
silence can't endure it either –
whatever breathes *time* breathes
and that abiding something-other
holds me like what holds those who

these seven-times-seven years
have clustered to their eerie
consolatory short story
that's everything a child *would* hope:
that a time comes, reappears,
that with a firm and measured step
it's all at once beside us

like seven-times-seven footsteps
along the sounding tunnel
as I walk this old canal.
And as often as I turn to see
who's there and they're my steps,
I think they're mine till somebody
goes past me without turning.

from *Times Literary Supplement*

The Ghosting Of Paul Celan

◇ ◇ ◇

In shadow from the past
I have tried to tell
of what the breath-crystal
in a word rejects:
greed of the eyes to see again,
greed of the fingers, all five.

Against the odds an image,
against the flow,
no pronouncements,
advancing –
                        Thicket, the image
lunges through the thicket
out there, in the head.

Firebomb and
martyrdom, how
neighbourly in sound, by wires
people move, Punch
and Black-Eyes. Wires twist
round cortex and ankle.

Slow image, painful, breathless:
in ordinary civvies
four or five of them,
seen from behind, four or five
dispersed, walk forward beneath
the living branches.

In the red gaze of wine
in its house of glass
there'll be sometimes a dragon;

sometimes a reminder
that trust is for the free,
the foolish, the very rare free.

Sliding through cropped grass
boots and shoes

and then the foreknown
about to happen, any moment
some unspeakable thing.

See then ways they mix
into the mutations. If we cringe,
the god will spit on us;
apprehend the tact while pipe and string
carry us away,
and in the music we are lost.

from *Poetry Review*

Salvage

◊   ◊   ◊

In years gone by and now again
the river's docile
tributaries swell, topple

banks like heifers clashing in the lane.
Hide-heavy water bodies fall
on fields of flood.

At the foot of walls
the turning waters leave
a mess of mirrors, puddle deep,

to show the ruined
complexion of the clouds
to one who sifts,

lifts broken branches or a gate to free
strayed geese, the buoyant
coop, a broody hen.

from *Times Literary Supplement*

Admit you feel like all the ice skates in Brazil

◇ ◇ ◇

left over from a trade agreement in the nineteenth century
and surely still upended in a locked room somewhere,
blades turned skyward, laces all untied.

Outside, it's 32 degrees. Disuse has made them
elegant. They've never sluiced a diagram
across a frozen lake. No one has drowned in them.

They've never held the slim feet of a lady
in a sable coat. At night, their sharpened edges
make strange arrows on the wall.

Imagine how they'd pinch the skin.
How neat they are. How many.
How they'd cut if they could.

from *Poetry London*

From 'Earth Records', 27

◇   ◇   ◇

The bitterness of British factories. Marx.
The day kicks off when night has yet to lift
its parka hood. You clock off in the dark.
Eight labouring hours to clamber up the cliff,
two more to climb the hill behind. Or flop
onto canteen seating between two shifts.
To feed the beasts whose needs will never stop,
sacrifice at the surplus megaliths.
No glaciers dragged those bricks to where they stand
on the plains as sunless temples to time,
but rollers hauled by teams of tiring hands,
a skin of cuts, accumulated grime.
A fair wind still brings the cotton and wool –
warm coats from hot lands where factories are full.

from *The Morning Star*

So Much Will Waste

◇　◇　◇

Flat on my back in a Methodist chapel
I watch a plastic bag fill up with blood.
It's mine, and next to me is you, and yours
is filling half as fast and twice as red.
I hate to state the obvious, but baby,
we're already lying down, and when it's done
they'll toss them both together in a van;
we'll never see those pints of us again,
and they're no longer ours – other men

will share you, other women me, the secrets
of our hearts will whisper in the walls
of strangers' ears. So by comparison,
we've known each other years in this position,
since we know our bodies, young and strong,
were vetted good to go. It's all the same –
our tissues sank, we both filled in the forms,
and we could brush in arteries or veins
as close as passengers on rush-hour trains.

We'll breathe and bruise, it hasn't killed us yet;
the window closing when the platelets clot
is thin as plasters, fragile as the Tuc they hand you
in the blush of standing up. But this is not
the closest we could get to how it feels to swim
across a body like a foreign cell: forget the spinning
ceiling, then, let steel mosquitoes dive towards
the wrists of noble citizens. They'll do no harm
that we can't heal in one another's arms.

from *The Erotic Review*

SEAN O'BRIEN

Thirteen O'Clocks

◇ ◇ ◇

Grey days, a late spring, and in theory
The administration falls
With a commonsense rattle
Of handed-back car-keys,
Grey days when 'ideology',
The stuff that forms the very walls
On which the roof has always rested,
Unfolds like origami in reverse
To leave a bare white page
Uncannily like 'ideology'.
Essayists stand at their windows. Uh.
Meanwhile no blood and no curfew,
No lamp-posts. Life could be worse.

★

Parks and Gardens, Ways and Means,
Drains, Finance and General Purposes
And all the virtuous tedium required
To underwrite the civil surfaces,
The lawns on which the lovers lie
As bands complacently reiterate
The glories of our blood and state:
It takes a backfire (was it?) from a car
To call to mind that where we are
Is only happenstance and not
The happy land that history forgot.
See where an aged theorist takes the air.
Another car backfires. Christ, it's hot.

★

The tidal range is almost nil. Deep gulfs
Far out, but at the coastline plains of mud
Lie there for novelists to contemplate.

'All geography is exile, like the self.'
Is this the kind of thing they mean by 'late'?

Hans X arrived here for a single summer.
Nothing happened and he died
Still slim in his white suit at eighty,
Dry as this salt-shrunken table.
                                    The wind
Picks up across low dunes, the sun
Goes down like clockwork, like maritime commerce,
Red-eyed and unfinished, into the salt.
A fate we may suppose is anyone's.

★

Sleep is for sale, not to the sleepless only,
Reading on or staring out the clock,

But to the shallow generality as well.
Deep blankness makes them look like amateurs.

How soon the consolations of the lamp, the wakeful
Silence of the wide waste night, will seem perverse
And be forbidden!
                        Pale insomniacs,
Mark a final page and like your sleeping partners

Learn to die a little. Let the bones unfix,
The mind vacate its premises, until
Your absence feels like home, and you can reap
The dividend of all this quiet industry
With coppers on your empty eyes.

★

These complicated assignations
At provincial railway stations
And low convenient hotels
Complete with other people's smells
Mean 'public life is dead in X.'
Therefore they concentrate on sex,
Where it is always afternoon.
They say transgression sets them free:
They would have done it anyway.
She's always late. He comes too soon.
Although there is a price to pay,
What can outbid complicity
And sitting on a train all day?

★

A kind of poetry, a kind of sex,
Dreamed up by Stone-Age Protestants
(Have it by heart and keep it in your pants).
You can't imagine where you'll find it next
But rest assured it hasn't gone away.
Discovered down the back of a settee
Or scattered loosely on a table. Rita
Hayworth, I have come to set you free
From being classified as 'X.'.
I am the President for life. My face
Is on the banknotes and my cheques
Are blanker than the bankrupt mind of God.
You'd like it really, Rita. Yes, you would.

★

Or the enormous range of afterwards,
The birchwoods and the endless marshes,
The grey sea and the greyer shore
Where you forget what drove you here.

Night falls. As one wave finishes
Another is preparing to arrive. The chalk roads
Turn to sand as economics vanishes.
This swamp was once a kingdom. We don't care.

We don't know from category error.
We just want to hate whoever's next –
Too rich, too philistine, too highly sexed.
The thing about the coast, it languishes.
Bring on the deluge and the reign of terror.

★

A yawning execution squad
Is mustered in the still-dark yard,
Unshaven and unbreakfasted
And for a moment hard to know
Apart from the condemned,
Who enter by another door,
A chorus of the unrehearsed
Who seem to have their roles by heart.
The difference you missed before
Is not the weapons only but the belts
That can hold up the trousers.

It was a different world, my friend,
One inaccessible to bourgeois art.
Do not suppose effects have causes.

★

Eternal afternoon, whose shadows play
Grandmother's footsteps as you look
Time in the face and quickly look away:
The clock examines you insatiably,
The moment of decision never ends.
Is this the prelude or the main event
And is the answer somewhere in a book,
Or will the signs be unmistakable
When you make history by being here,
Not there to hear the shouting on the stairs?
Is waiting in itself the true occasion,
And have you failed rise to it so far,
And who exactly do you think you are?

★

Please stress the second syllable: e-*vil*,
When speaking of the hour that has come
That no one quite believed and no one doubted.

Grim glamour of its ordinariness!
It has the look you dream it will –
Street furniture, the lamp-posts' curlicues, heat-haze
On boulevards that have not been diverted –

At once like home and what you should not see,
The present, nothing more and nothing less,
Whose psychopathic citizens
May go abroad about their business,
Taking their cue from something in the air
To greet the end of days.

★

When all else fails, it must be murder.
The city's calm, with this in mind. The state
Will yield no other remedy. There is
A thirteenth hour after all. The lime-trees
March in close formation to the gate
And then beyond into the eastern haze.
Somewhere the final order is restored.
Knee-deep in our true element,
We catch the scent of blood and excrement
And the incinerated libraries
Of those who had it coming. We are home
In time to hear the cherry blossom
Thunder on the empty streets.

from *Poem*

RICHARD OSMOND

The Well

◇ ◇ ◇

Sometimes I read Hopkins and think, 'It's grand, but what did you make all that noise for? It sounds like someone throwing hammers down a well.'

As Adam, new-made, in naming struck
his will against the green, native nature of things,
I hammered hard and happy, tapping the stuck
        stiff rope-reel of the well
            into its proper sprocket, singing
            the while in concert, mechanic-
-al, with the crank, which, hit, knelled bell-
like, loud, until the mallet, sweaty, slipped and fell.

    Foul metal rattle, clattering down
            into hell's bowels, clapper of sound
        uncontrolled and clanging, it
                rang as this song does, tumbling
on itself and by its noise all meaning numbing.
I, slack workman, would
that I'd a lesson learned of good
        craft and fit-
                tempered tuning
        from the anvil-branded
    pitch of Pythagoras' tenet
(any man who, walking by the blacksmiths, understands
    the high harmony of hammers held in hand,
        not loosed and lost down wells, already knows it)
    but alas, my tool is fallen beyond fetch of winch or bucket.
    I cannot reach. No more can I retract, as wrong, my rash allit-
    -eration than Adam into Eden re-admit.

from *The Literateur*

RUTH PADEL

from *The Okazaki Fragments*

◊   ◊   ◊

i
First Cell

Born in a deepsea vent, synthesized
by lightning in a reducing atmosphere
or carried here by meteorite. Algae, first
self-replicating molecule on Earth,

pulls carbon from organic substrate,
performs the world's first magic,
photo-synthesis of air to oxygen,

and creates copies of herself, uncountable
as starlings flocking or the pure gold bricks
Sheba sent to Solomon by mule.

Cell in the air, on the rocks. Song
hoping to be heard in a heart cut open.
Little Blue-Green, dreaming of pattern
and form. Tiny horseman of apocalypse.

iv
Entry of the Membrane

We lose and find ourselves. Eukaryotes
have taken over, sequestering
those riotous organelles in an interior
pillowcase of lipid gift-wrap. Tissue
redefines the nucleus, blocks leakage
from one chamber to another
and coils in the DNA
like diaphanous kernmantle rope.

A new design, communicating
with world outside
through a new-minted retina
so *Out* can safely come *In*. For the first time
Earth is seen. Shafts of winter sunlight
flicker in fissured evergreen.

vi
Pairs

We've left the unstable world of RNA
and wobble base pairs behind.
You can't rely on a single strand.
Come in double ply new-fangledness
of DNA, macromolecule
whose ribose boasts one atom less
of oxygen. My love meet me half way:
pairing inside comes quick
as romance, as electric shock.
Cytosine claims Guanine as a bride
en bloc. Adenine makes a play
for Thymine the wild girl,
awkward, fresh from school.

viii
Dealing the Chromosomes

Bodies stained with colour. Shadow stripes
like a multi-storey against a city's sky
at night, transporting DNA in careful order.

It can't be just crammed in like a ball of string
so here they are: flags on the road to self, chromatin
folded in like egg-white. Forty-six of them

packed in the nucleus as in a Christmas stocking.
One-from-him-and-one-from-her, in pairs:
traits you later think are yours. Limp hair,

an allergy to lanolin, a tendency to make
the odd rash choice, deal cards
with your left hand. Shades of your voice.

Breaking the Bond

Cell summons ATP, Adenosine Triphosphate
Who coins and hoards all energy, to break
those welded rungs and separate the partners
in their hydrogen-bond pavane.

Got to be done. Like snapping a bone
to re-set it. Then Helicase the Unwinder,
motor protein, zooms through nucleic acid
backbone, tickles buds of replication

and tugs apart the annealed strands
like spiral fronds of honeysuckle whose stems,
sheltering that nest of wrens you watched
hatch out last spring, have grown together

hardening into wood, for years. Helicase spins
DNA like a turbo till replication forks appear
just where you'd say they never could: in
the filofax of the nucleus. Splitting, then copying, begins.

from *Poem*

Pow

◊ ◊ ◊

Though I think of you   eating three tiny chicken hearts on a skewer
or the skinny girl at school   with shallow breathing and white hands,
chicken-hearted means easily frightened, and has nothing to do with the heart.

A Crown prince is a male heir to a sovereign throne.   A Crown princess
is the wife of a Crown prince.

Though I think of opening our door to a postman we were told had died
the month before,   postman's knock is a game where imaginary letters
are exchanged for kisses
                         and has nothing to do with dead men at the door.

Inner man – the soul or mind, the stomach.   For inner woman see
INNER MAN.   Camelopard is not a hybrid of a camel and a leopard.

Though I think of a line of cow hearts   strung up by the
side of a road in Kochin, swarming with flies, their tubes open to the sky   like
bird mouths,   a purple heart is nothing but an amphetamine
tablet or a US military decoration.

Simplicity   is a rainbird.   A rainbird is a bird that can forewarn of rain.

Butter-and-eggs is not butter and eggs,   but a plant with two shades of yellow in
its flower.   Daffodil, toadflax, bunny mouths, dead men's bones,
impudent lawyer, Jacob's ladder, lion's mouth, snapdragon.

Though I am listing flowers   I am not thinking of flowers.

from *Poetry London*

Sainte-Chapelle

◊　◊　◊

Just as a master glassmaker must rest the iron blowpipe
against his cheek between blows, so as not to suck
the flame into his mouth when he draws breath,

so must you let the sun pierce your window
and rest against your face. It also is a furnace,
one of many in the sky's workshop,

yet the earth lets sunrays rest along its cheek,
drawing just what it needs to paint in light.
I tell you this after visiting La Sainte-Chapelle,

as you lie on your less painful lung, only
half-listening, concentrating on each inhalation.
But I persist, as if I could conjure the fifteen

fifty-foot-high stained-glass windows in your flat,
sand grain by sand grain, each grisaille detail
fused at impossible temperatures. I tell you

how cobalt can be added to raw glass to make blue,
copper for red and green, antimony for yellow.
How the panes are held in place

with lead cames and iron rods. How they have withstood
a revolution and eight centuries of storms.
It doesn't matter that the trefoils and medallions

illustrate the bible and you are not a believer,
that there are fire-horses, a golden calf, plagues, wars.
The history of our species is up in that chapel.

As you lie there sleeping, the radiant colours
play over the altar of your skin
while the oxygen pump chugs its hymn.

from *Poetry London*

HEATHER PHILLIPSON

Rumination on 25mm of Cotton

◇ ◇ ◇

It's the hammerless C-string of the world's stupid piano.
Between my left and right hand, above the covers

whipped up like the Urals, it's the rope over an abyss.
It's a travesty of hand-stitching, a decapitation.

Whose cotton limb? It dangles from my thumb
and forefinger. The universe slackens in its shadow.

Sir, Herr, Monsieur, Dottore, M'Lord,
Your Honour – I tore it from its felted home

in palsy-walsy boredom. The long sound of the wind /
the hypnotic high-pitch / a rhapsody from the alley.

Or it was the spoutings of small whales on asphalt
carried via mothballs in the wardrobe.

For a moment, the thread was immense. I plucked it. Hard.
Mute hint of our bond with fluff, it hangs in night's unbound girdle.

from *Poetry London*

Girl at the World's End

◊ ◊ ◊

You're probably in a band
with black in its name.

Some exquisite drone,
with a tiny – but dedicated – following.

Unimpeachably hip.
Hair: a perfect Siouxsie mess.

Instead of standing at the bar
you sag.

Sabbath. Angels. Mountain.
Keys. Lips. Flag.

from *Rising*

KATE POTTS

Thirty-three

◊ ◊ ◊

Now all the boys I've loved are married off, ensconced.
They bide in milky, clean-hewn terraces, in replicated seaside towns.

They wear matched socks. They wash. They see their own fathers' chins
and petulance – the kindnesses and tics – grow strong

and coarse in them, and this is comfort. They lullaby
their round-faced wives in lusty, baritone, newsreader voices.

Pour me a slug of this late August clarity of light: the contrast turned up high –
blunt as bone, acerbic as our windfall apples.

The garden's overrun with teetering foxgloves, cigarette ends, soup tins,
broken televisions; luscious, hoary, interloping weeds.

A fat fox grazes the rubbish sacks. Cars lope, tacit, by the kerb.
I hold my breath in tightly and bless the motoring

wish, wish of my pulse. On TV, the newsreader speaks of riots. His voice
is muffled pips and swells – is someone underwater.

from *Poetry Review*

No Touching

◇   ◇   ◇

I would like to ruin your life
let it not be said I lack the necessary
imagination to be jealous
I would ask you to tell no one about us
and if you tell no one about us
I'll fight hard to hide my disappointment
I would like you to renounce your past
as quite a big mistake
it will mean something although I
will never completely forgive you
I think you represent
the possibility in my life of renewal
I would like people to say
'she came back a different person'
we will appear at the weddings
of people we don't care about
our faces radiant from fucking

from *Clinic*

After a Line by George Seferis

◊　◊　◊

The time came, and the dogs tore him to pieces.
Or it came and they rested their muzzles on his lap,
or it came with such stealth he slept through it.

Hindsight favours what becomes, and the past
concurs, shrugs into line behind the love affair,
the sickness unto death, the sudden lapse,

which now must seem inevitable, ever there,
the way a swift incursion in the night will show
that your city lay as open as a split fig.

And the hounds, those feral packs that took their cues
from fate, and did its work, primed to rear up
at a finger-snap, mere bone-meal now.

Euripides, whose throat we hear they tore,
was killed by winter's chill, betrayal, long before
the dogs burst from their dark, wet groves.

from *The Rialto*

Finding the Keys

◊ ◊ ◊

The set seed and the first bulbs showing.
The silence that brings the deer.

The trees are full of handles and hinges;
you can make out keyholes, latches in the leaves.

Buds tick and crack in the sun, break open
slowly in a spur of green.

★

The small-change colours of the river bed:
these stones of copper, silver, gold.

The rock-rose in the waste-ground
finding some way to bloom. The long

spill of birdsong. Flowers, all
turned to face the hot sky. Nothing stirs.

★

That woody clack of antlers.
In yellow and red, the many griefs of autumn.

The dawn light through amber leaves
and the trees are lanterned, blown

the next day to empty stars.
Smoke in the air; the air, turning.

★

Under a sky of stone and pink
faring in from the north and promising snow:

the blackbird.
In his beak, a victory of worms.

The winged seed of the maple,
the lost keys under the ash.

from *Poetry London*

nsfw

◇ ◇ ◇

i'm sick of love & sad for what I've lost:
that bullshit fix of nervy hands has gone &
rude spring's a bully, sun & wavy cold air
& you are well, i having never been well i,
i want to meet you anew and be loved &
not thought of as silly – to you now i'm
a clown or a dog waiting to be put down
& so my breasts are hairy teats for cubs i love
& are not born, & not for you, my new nude
is atrocious & i wonder who you
think of in the shower, what wets your meat
if not my putrid body you once & gently
fucked & which i, promising it to you, have lost
the receipt for. go away for a long time

& meet me at the airport, run me a bath
as before with water from the kettle so
kind & we'll shiver in two inches forever,
thigh on thigh never shrinking from the
moment but cycling it around the time
we do have, having been given each other, &
never unadorned or waiting to get broke.
i'd wait to die forever to have unlost
that time & die to lose it all again,
having taken too much, having got
love unspent not wanted & staid unhappy
inside the kettle waiting to be filled kindly,
touched on the cunt or met at the airport with the
ghosts of animal kingdoms still inside me.

from *Jacket*

CHARLOTTE RUNCIE

Lothian Road, Saturday Night

◊　◊　◊

'hi we danced . . . i left, u got ur bag
sorry i didnt speak outside my mate was going fighting

me blonde hair

u black top'

　　　– a Missed Connections listing on gumtree.com

Outside rain flared the sparks that dripped
from hogmanay rockets lit over us,
scattered in haar that reached across
to sob on seven shoulders.

Cold winced around. Your shirt disintegrated,
beer-transparent laced with air.

We could have stayed until the gun,
but you hungered for the heat
of a connecting punch.

I got my bag. You gone,
I walked among the stone
shocked wet as if you'd smacked it,

the tenements crackling with paint spot lights
dragged into stars by a drunk eye's toothpick.

from *Edinburgh Review*

DECLAN RYAN

From Alun Lewis

◊　◊　◊

There is nothing that can save today, darling,
you not being here. You MUST write.
It's impossible to breathe otherwise.
I'm only talking of the things I really NEED.
I'm so tired of travelling away from you.
I think of you all the bloody time. Do you mind?

This isn't an answer or a letter –
it's only a cup of coffee after lunch.
Many things I've been unable to remember
came to me last night.
You sitting like a babu at a desk
in the bowels of the G.P.O.
You standing in the quartier latin corridor
of the Hotel Marina on Sunday afternoon
after the cinema saying 'Alright, pay the taxi. Let's stay.'

When I saw you on Saturday July 24th
you were the flash of a sword.
Now I'm hopelessly shut into the camp life again.
A soccer match, a disjointed conversation at dinner,
a visit to the reading room to see how things go:
oh and a longing beyond words.

There's a fat dove strutting across the lawn
by the bougainvillea.
I wish I could be strolling with you
looking at the rose moles all in stipple
in your little stream.
One way or another I make a lot of shadows where I go.

Don't worry over the hairs on my head.
May you not be tried harder than you can bear.
Let there be an again, New Year. Save us.

from *Poetry Review*

The Revenant

◊ ◊ ◊

Downhill . . . and I met myself,
a pale ghost glimmering
the way a poacher's torch shines
there – now there – between the trees

so it seems at moments as if
they too are ghosts, walking
in a new light, coming
out of memory towards you . . .

When we met, myself and I,
each cast the other into a kind
of shining shadow,

my younger self ascending through me
like a shiver, as I turned
toward the house below.

from *The New Statesman*

CAMELLIA STAFFORD

I will stay at home and talk on the telephone

◊ ◊ ◊

It's tricky to explain what I'm up to these days,
whose dawns snap like the polystyrene cups
I cracked to seed beads in the King's cafeterias,
as you checked my pulse and said things like,
today, your aura is apricot.

I am hidden at the end of the last ring
before I pick up. My voice transpires over
a battery. I stay at home and talk of hem
lengths, paper bouquets to my faraway sister.
Toy with the idea you will call me

from the pay phone at your old shared house,
Turnpike Lane, knelt on the floor by a blot
of silvers and coppers, satisfying sounds
of their clatter through our powwows,
when we said things like, *paradiso e inferno!*

Many late nights, you fell asleep on the line,
after hours of talking in the bar, the library,
our apres-class jinks around Covent Garden.
I never hung up but sometimes I woke you.
Others, I stayed quiet.

from *Magma*

The Paris Poems

◊ ◊ ◊

I.

from the metro entrances
greenery-yallery light
mantles upwards, seems to
hesitate

at the sight of rain and
the unnatural poor

II.

rumour has it:
in the fountains dusty birds
are laving

one feather and
then another feather splayed, needling,
one whole wing

and then one whole white bird

III.

the rain presses her spitty
bubbling lips to each rue saint–denis
house

that's the rumour, the rumour that history
loves us

IV.

give history
a kiss where the grime is thinnest

some sort of peace, yes,
if we take down the resistance memorials
which disturb

V.

in the morning, some lucky people
including me
receive stays of execution

the bakery opens and
citizens are
taking yellow loaves away
in their paper sheaths

VI.

having found shelter, I try out sadness

again
and again this bloodless anointing, strange scent
on the wrist

from *Cake*

Songlines

◊   ◊   ◊

Timing is all, and as your eyes move along
the page, like a typewriter, pressing the return
key, you begin to hear the riff of time's song-

lines, filling up, taking over. So you turn
round and, there in the mirror, you find a script
written without your permission, which, you learn,

is the script of your life in progress, a life stripped
from you and turned into a pattern that is more
pattern than you'd like, stricter, more tight-lipped

more revealing . . .
. . . But then, you ask, how can we restore
the body into its shapes, send the music
of time into reverse? Is there a way to score

music so it holds us in eternity in some classic
frozen moment? Are the shapes we discover behind
our backs capable of movement – jerkily physic-

al, broken, like this line – into ourselves, refined
like oil, or gold? Or, say, a hand, two eyes,
a mouth, each fine detail singing in an unlined

unwritten poetry that takes everyone by surprise,
the street itself moving in time, its music faint
but relentless, of happening, of song-lines as cries.

from *Kaffeeklatsch*

HELEN TOOKEY

Portrait of a Young Woman

◇   ◇   ◇

This morning, the moon's volte-face as
the month changed handedness, the right

profile sharp against sky, the left
dissolving in shadow at nape

and jawline – gestures rehearsed by
Leonardo contemplating

surface and stylus, movements of
hand and mind this unknown face makes

legible, its sweeps of grace and
energy always from rightward

edge extending infinitely
into leftward space, structuring

a grammar shared through this half-month,
etched in this new moon's metalpoint.

from *Poetry Wales*

Fetish

◇   ◇   ◇

'I . . . expressed the hope that he, in making a limping girl happy, might himself become happy.'

Case 46, *Psychopathia Sexualis*, Dr R von Krafft-Ebing

You are a
catastrophic
assemblage,
a random
agglomeration
of tics and
properties,
aggregated
erogenata,
eyes, teeth,
cosmetics
and nostrils,
late cubist
masterpiece
demanding
obeisance,
wild voudou
writhing and
self-abjurance.
Perspective
lost, I submit
to your skull
rattle, blood
drum thumping
ecstasis.

from *Rising*

Collaboration

◊   ◊   ◊

At 4 p.m. Manning and I had sat down to discuss the poem
and his role in it. An imaginary wind buffeted and rattled
the remote French farmhouse window like some sort of
device, a signifier of something trenchant and solemn.
Manning said he was so excited about the poem that he was
actually *rock-hard* as he put it, and what about I set it in a
hotel room and sort him out with a Latvian stripper and half
an ounce of good quality gak. And then quite matter-of-factly,
he pulled his johnson out of his zoot suit pants to show me
his predicament. His member (though my gaze, I can assure
you, recoiled from it with more haste than a hand would from
a hot coal) looked something like a monstrous jewel in the
setting of the surrounding grey fabric of his trousers; or like,
perhaps, a misplaced floral buttonhole that would have
seemed less offensive had it protruded from the suit's lapel.
It seemed to me that its grotesque rudeness buzzed against its,
dare I say it, rather feminine beauty with a metallic ringing
sound, but perhaps that was merely tinnitus brought on by the
stress of the situation. I'd never known Manning to talk or
behave in this way before. And even though it soon came to
me that he'd been suffering from concussion after being hit
full on the head by a lance in a jousting accident, and even
though within a day or so he'd recover fully and return to his
sensitive, and innately feminist self, I found that I always felt
a little wary in his presence thereafter, for what I'd heard and
seen that afternoon must surely have lain dormant in him for
all the time I'd known him. And perhaps since then, I
consequently feel a little less secure in the company of all my
friends and acquaintances as well, of course, as in the
company of myself.

from *Kaffeeklatsch*

NERYS WILLIAMS

The Thirteen Club

After Michael Collins's The Likes of Us:
A Biography of the White Working Class

◊   ◊   ◊

Take me to the thirteenth door
to the home of thirteen tables.

Dressed in green ties
we touch skeleton pins at our button holes.

Leave your shoes on the table
open your umbrellas (above your heads, please).

The cross-eyed waiters know where to look
serving a crash of broken mirrors.

Enter under this ladder
see the cat braided with peacock feathers.

Spill your salt before you eat
step on a crack to break your mother's back.

Somebody's walking on my future grave.
Should I knock on wood
before crows peck at windows?

You touch your brow
mumbling an aphorism for philanthropy.

Just for luck.

from *Poetry Wales*

CONTRIBUTORS' NOTES AND COMMENTS

RACHAEL ALLEN co-runs the anthology and event series *Clinic*. Her poems have appeared or are forthcoming in *The Sunday Times*, *Poetry London* and *Dear World and Everyone In It* (Bloodaxe). She is currently studying at the University of East Anglia. She writes: 'I am interested in the ideas of the skewed landscape and how we work to defamiliarise what is familiar to us, and conversely, how we work to recognise something known made unfamiliar. I wanted the poem to revolve around the scene I was attempting to articulate as though circling it. The poem is a journey from a supermarket in my home-town in Cornwall to the small area of scrubby wasteland behind it, cut through by a motorway. Many people from the town would camp on this scrubland and attempt to use it as a semi-wilderness, a large garden, where there would be parties and gatherings. The idea of the lush, cultivated wildness of the garden contrasted strongly for me with the plastic yellow of the supermarket, and how one could accommodate the other felt astonishing to both constructs; the signs of the supermarket to the people camping signified a new kind of light – a new moon – working to light the area in such a way that I could just about recognise it. This poem was my attempt to recognise it.'

EMILY BERRY grew up in London and studied English Literature at Leeds University and Creative Writing at Goldsmiths College. An Eric Gregory Award winner in 2008, she is a contributor to *The Breakfast Bible*, a compendium of breakfasts published by Bloomsbury. Her debut poetry collection is *Dear Boy*, published by Faber & Faber. She comments: 'An internal conflict arises whenever I am asked to say something explicatory about one of my poems. I sit down and try to do it – I write many unconnected sentences and half-sentences beginning with things like "It seems . . ." and "It may be that . . .". I want to comply and do a good job because the instinct to be well-behaved is strong, but a sort of writery impotence has descended on me. I can tell you some basic facts. "Arlene's House" is a sort of sequel to "Sweet Arlene" (which appeared in *Best British Poetry 2011*), if poems can have sequels. A reviewer of the collection in which both poems appear likened them to a "recurring bad dream". This seems a good description. They are poems about fear – the kind of fear that arises from what Freud called the *Unheimliche* (the uncanny), when the familiar becomes unfamiliar. I've called upon the poem to justify itself beyond this, or at least introduce itself in straight-forward terms but it has retreated somewhere beyond my reach (or I've purposely sent it off). Maybe what happened was I was held captive by the editors of *Best British Poetry 2013* and I begged them to let me ring my poem, promising to trick it into giving itself up, but when the poem answered I shouted "*Save yourself – run!!!*" before the editors had a chance to snatch the phone off me and hold a Stanley knife to my throat.'

LIZ BERRY was born in the Black Country. She received an Eric Gregory Award in 2009 and her pamphlet *The Patron Saint of Schoolgirls was* published by Tall-Lighthouse in 2010. Her debut collection will be published by Chatto & Windus in 2014. She writes: 'Bird' is a poem about the thrilling, terrifying, sometimes painful, process of transformation, of becoming something new, something you've longed for.

My sister and I were the first girls in our family to have the chance to stay on in education and to move away from home. Our family was fiercely proud of us and I knew how hard they'd worked to make it possible. My mom used to say that she thought of her daughters as birds – push them out of the nest to fly when they're ready and trust that they'll find their way back to you. I realise now what an extraordinary gift that was and how it took a great deal of love and bravery. The girl in the poem can be bold and full of nerve because her family cheer her on: larks sing with her mother's voice, her grandmother waves her off from the fode. As she takes flight for the first time, the Black Country and all its birds are alongside her, lifting her upwards and on.'

PATRICK BRANDON's first collection, *A Republic of Linen* (Bloodaxe), was published 2009. He won the Essex Poetry Prize in 2005, and received commendations in the Wigtown Poetry Prize 2005 and the National Poetry Competition 2007. He received a New Writing Ventures bursary in 2006. He is also a practicing artist and exhibits regularly. He lives in Bristol with his partner and two children. He writes this on his poem: 'The poem takes its name and cue from a painting by Rene Magritte (*L'Esprit de géométrie*, 1937), in which the artist exchanges the heads of a mother and baby. The poem is loosely ekphrastic in that the image is the starting point for the poem. The poem does not describe the painting, but it does touch upon the same giddy shift in relationship from natural to uncanny, drawing attention to an intimate bond rather than merely depicting a narcissistic world in which fathers dress up and coiffure their sons to look like smaller versions of themselves. The playground for the child is a place for constant reinvention. For the parent too it can be a joyful world, but it can also a place of melancholy and insufferable repetition – especially when cold and wet.'

JAMES BROOKES was born in 1986 and grew up in rural Sussex, a few minutes' walk from Shelley's boyhood home of Field Place. He received a major Eric Gregory Award in 2009 and a Hawthornden International Writer's Fellowship in 2011. He has published a pamphlet, *The English Sweats*, with Pighog Press and is currently the Williams Librarian at Cranleigh School in Surrey, where also he teaches. *Sins of the Leopard*, his first full collection was published by Salt in 2012.

He comments: 'The raw stuff of the poem owes to Allen Peterson, the American poet to whom it is dedicated. 'That Silver that Bone' is a poem in his collection *Anonymous Or* (Defined Providence Press, 2002). I was reading all I could of his remarkable work when I came upon the "Amen – Artillery" volume of an American English dictionary in the HG Wells public house in Worcester Park, London. Thanks are therefore due to the British poet Phil Brown for holding his birthday celebrations there in 2011. The poem first appeared on the website of *The White Review*; Roddy Lumsden then sharpened its lines in the course of editing *Sins of the Leopard*. I much prefer the later version, which feels less dense and lifts the ideas off the larynx just enough to let the poem breathe. It would be easy to say that the poem takes after Kierkegaard's *Fear and Trembling*, or that it suggests that the use of language itself requires a teleological suspension of the ethical. That would be a neat an explanation; far too neat. What higher certainty of purpose do we hope excuses our actions anyway? I don't see any political edge to that question which does not also apply itself to the vitals of writing.'

SAM BUCHAN-WATTS is a postgraduate student at the University of East Anglia and lives in London. He is a co-editor of the *Clinic* anthology series and has contributed to *Five Dials* and *New Walk*. He writes, 'The phrase "Nose to Tail" is distracting the name of a fashionable culinary concept and cookbook, which – almost fetishisticly, it seems – aims to utilize every inch of the animal. For a long time I figured it meant that the animals were simply touching standing with all of their limbs still attached, as though forming an orderly queue.

The epigraph is based loosely on a short, very upsetting PETA animal welfare documentary about factory farming, "Meet Your Meat", narrated by Alec Baldwin. I came to this via David Foster Wallace's 2004 essay for *Gourmet* magazine, "Consider the Lobster", which includes the famous straw-man question "is it all right to boil a sentient creature alive just for our gustatory pleasure?" And I'm 100% with Wallace in that I'm "concerned not to come off as shrill or preachy when what I really am is a little confused". I've never had the desire to write with an ecological agenda, purely because the imperative in any poem is to interrogate or query rather than change.

Wallace's essay closes – like the best poems – with a set of questions, and no attempt to answer them definitively. The queries arc out into the broad issue of measuring aesthetics against morality. I hope the two may nudge against each other here, as the pigs do in their endless distracted stack of other smiling pigs.'

HAYLEY BUCKLAND was born in 1977. She graduated from Norwich School of Art and Design in 2005 and completed an MA in Creative Writing at UEA in 2006. Her work has since appeared in a variety of publications and competitions, including *Mslexia*, *Magma* and *Poetry Review*. She lives and works in Norwich as a freelance writer and is currently involved with functional skills work with teenagers at risk of exclusion.

She writes: 'I've always loved the Ranunculus flower. They are small blooms with very tightly packed delicate petals, almost like crepe paper. The flower head is dense, but when it starts to wilt, the petals droop down around the central stem so that it looks like a downturned mouth or baggy "jowls" around a "nose". I think they look hilarious in the vase, like a collection of incontinent, moaning old women, and I leave them much longer than other flowers after they've turned. The poem began as an extension of mood relating to the slight bitterness or dissatisfaction that can hang in the air between two people. The personification of the flowers, and the twig at the window, suggest an audience to help highlight the ridiculousness of the bickering that often occurs between couples as they do something simple like cook a meal. We can all be childish and ratty and would probably be embarrassed if anyone overheard. The poem mixes the elements of domesticity, nature and a certain energy that is difficult to pinpoint or keep control over, both in real life and on the page.'

HARRY BURKE is a writer based in London. His poems have been published in *Clinic* and *Stop Sharpening Your Knives*. He comments, 'This poem first appeared in a series of poems I wrote under the title "Junkspace", which was loosely derived from Rem Koolhaas's observation that "*If* space-junk is the *human debris* that litters the universe *Junk-Space* is the residue mankind leaves on the planet." Koolhaas's essay of the same name (from 2001) is an architectural treatise advocating the creation of meaning out of the spaces between other spaces. It's about creating new meaning within pre-existing configurations. Koolhaas wrote this in the context of architecture but it seems appropriate for poetry also. The series is mostly abandoned now and I've lost the html somehow :(.

This poem was written at a time when all poems were about falling in love, and some were about collapse. Now it's the other way round. If you turn the poem on its side it's a stock market chart.'

JOHN BURNSIDE's most recent collection, *Black Cat Bone*, won the Forward and the T.S. Eliot Prizes. He teaches at St Andrews University. He writes: '"At the Entering of the New Year" was inspired by a remark by the great baseball player and coach, Yogi Berra: "The future isn't what it used to be". I have always loved Yogi's odd phrases and snippets of wisdom, (on being in the outfield at Yankee stadium, for example: "It gets late early out there", though my favourite of his observations may be: "In theory there is no difference between theory and practice. In practice there is"); several of the poems in my work in progress are inspired by the great man. The other influence is Thomas Hardy, from whom the poem's title is taken. I found Hardy was something of a presence behind the writing of my new book, not in terms of style, but in mood, in a certain sensibility. There is an air of stoicism in the book, which to some extent expresses dismay with the failings of humanity, (myself included, I hasten to add) but also gives voice to something else, a sense of enduring pleasure and a recognition of the significance of the more-than-human, the natural world in all its facets, and a recognition that our lives unfold in ways we do not understand, though we are capable of recognising that they are part of a larger narrative.'

MATTHEW CALEY's *Thirst* (Slow Dancer, 1999) was nominated for The Forward Prize for Best First collection. His most recent books – *Professor Glass* (Donut) and *Apparently* (Bloodaxe) have both been featured on BBC Radio 3's *The Verb*. He has recently read at The National Portrait Gallery for both the Lucien Freud Memorial readings and in association with The Lost Prince Exhibition, and talked on ee cummings at The Royal Festival Hall as part of their America/The Rest Is Noise season. He lives and writes in London. He says: '"My Beloved" is from on-going work "Rake" (noun and verb) – which might be described as "the oblique diary of a time-travelling rake" or of a pack (proper collective noun) of such rakes. One sixth of a six-sonnet string, it's a mono-rhymed monologue. One objective of Haussmann's boulevards was military – to get troops across the city quickly (to quell riots etc) but had many "secondary" effects: speeding up the city, connecting the rich and poor areas; and for commerce – out of them grew the arcades, forerunners of our hyper-markets. Baudelaire famously described his mistresses' eyes "lit up like shops to lure their trade". Here, the boulevard comes between lovers. (Incidental detail: I often tend to conflate Brixton and Paris. The "kerb" in this poem is probably in Brixton, but the boulevard is in Paris.)

Whilst it's man speaking to woman – gender shouldn't be too fixed – both protagonists get "pregnant" after all, phallo-centrism is lampooned, the word merde is a feminine rhyme (it can mean shit! and/or good luck!) and "man-to-woman" poems (and vice-versa) often hijack that genre for other purposes – animus v anima? All this is probably beside the point – my latest, provisional definition of a poem is the smell that words give off beyond meaning. (Incidental detail: Benjamin is a stately tree – weeping fig – usually planted by wide roads, roots often undermining them. It can stave off formaldehyde. Benzoin gum is used in perfume. Sean O'Brien in *The Deregulated Muse* compares Muldoon/Carson's use of the word as pun or quiddity. I blatantly nick that as both.) If all this seems too weighty for so slight a thing, or grants it a "depth via hindsight", that's the inevitable pitfall of writing about your own stuff. Forgive! Few of these ideas were on my mind as I wrote it – and I'm properly confident it's probably about something else entirely. You tell me.'

NIALL CAMPBELL is a poet from the Western Isles of Scotland. He has been a recipient of an Eric Gregory Award and a Robert Louis Stevenson Fellowship. His work has been previously published in magazines and anthologies including: *The Dark Horse, Granta, Poetry Review* and *Best Scottish Poems 2011*. He writes: "On Eriskay' was written for a relative who had reached an age where she was now 'older than old'. Visiting her I was reminded, in a strange, tangential way, of Borges's introduction to his *Book of Imaginary Beasts* where he wrote (and I paraphrase) that though there are infinite possibilities for the mythological creature – the body of an X with the head of a Y with the arms of a Z – that only a few of these 'beings' truly resonate with us – and these are the ones that point towards something in our inner selves. Here is where the Kelpie came in for me. The Kelpie is a Scottish mythical being that can transform between two shapes (a human and a horse) and I thought about those two parts that are us – the person: their character, their voice and mannerisms; and then the other part, the animal: our day-to-day, our heavy flesh. And what happens if the latter outlives the former. I wanted the poem to be about a love and a mourning for a thing that had gone but that is somehow still there.'

IAN CARTLAND was born in Derbyshire and lives in Cambridge. His work has been included in a number of UK magazines. He comments: 'Blindness is something I'd guess most people think about rarely, yet is something we can't help but find profoundly resonant. The very idea can induce paranoid empathetic fear in the sighted, and is in many ways affecting – sight carries a whole world of philosophical and emotional weight, totem bearer for the senses, for the primal roots of human experience. I wanted to evoke some part of this through the portrayal of a woman who is in various senses isolated, who is determined, assertive, of strong imagination, and who desires above all else to conceive a child. The sequence is intended to leave more room for the reader than would a wholly straightforward narrative, and throughout I've employed or juxtaposed related notions of superstition, ritual, longing, arbitrary nature and scientific surety. One thing is the relationship between fate, the 'arbitrary nature' of disease and the "sureties" of medical science – the name of the figure rhetorically addressed, Trachomatis, is taken not from mythology but from the bacterium responsible for a well-known infection that can lead to infertility and which remains one of the major causes of blindness in the world (though fortunately on the decline recently). As for the form, with its varying gaps and indentation, it seemed to fall into place quite readily to suit the content – it goes some way to counterbalance the underlying metrical and lyrical style of the text and, I hope, gives it sufficient room to breathe.'

MELANIE CHALLENGER is the author of one collection of poems, *Galatea* (Salt: 2006), and one work of non-fiction, *On Extinction* (Granta: 2011). She is currently a visiting scholar at the Hannah Arendt Center at Bard College, where she is completing her second book of prose. She writes: 'At the time that this poem was written, very quickly and naturally, I was spending nearly half of every day on the beach with my infant son. The poem concerns itself with the image of a child hurling a daffodil into the sea. The act is one that the observer can't penetrate. It suggests a gift to the gods. It also suggests a casual disposal of something and its irretrievability. It brought to mind a recurring dream I used to have as a child in which a car drove me away from my mother, who stood on the pavement weeping. I must have dreamed it a hundred times over the course of many years, until finally, mercifully, it stopped. The dream returned to me while I was caring for my own child because so much of the early years of child-rearing are about the gentle handling of advancing stages of loss. It's not necessarily an unhappy loss but it's one that provokes strong, mixed emotions. I included a private reference to the dream in the poem on the assumption that the sense of loss and the image of the car are sufficiently clear and universal to become more than an individual's experience or memory.'

KAYO CHINGONYI was born in Zambia in 1987, moving to the UK in 1993. He holds a BA in English Literature from The University of Sheffield and an MA in Creative Writing from Royal Holloway, University of London and works as a writer, events producer, and creative writing tutor. His poems have been published in a range of magazines and anthologies and in a debut pamphlet entitled *Some Bright Elegance* (Salt, 2012).

He has also been invited to read from his work at venues and events across the UK and internationally. He comments as follows: 'The N Word' is part of a longer work that I started writing in an indignant mood in response to a type of poem that Major Jackson calls, in his essay 'A Mystifying Silence: Big and Black', a poem of racial 'encounter' (in which a white speaker has their comfort arrested by the mere presence of a black person about whom they make judgements based on assumption). In particular I was angry because such poems are often failures of imagination though they are successful in other ways (take Sharon Olds's poem 'On The Subway' with its precise use of chromatic imagery or Tony Hoagland's manipulations of transgressive sentiment – in poems such as 'The Change' – in order to put the topic of race firmly on the table).

What bothers me isn't that such poems exist but that they reaffirm a racial paradigm that fixes 'whiteness' as the normative position from which 'otherness' is a privation (even as they purport to say something 'daring' about race). That is how the long poem 'calling a spade a spade' began. Both as a riposte to such poems but also as an attempt to shift the perspective from which such poems, or rather the binaries they perpetuate, view race. At this point it seems apt to share two epigraphs that I hope will precede the completed poem in print:

'I no longer write white writing/ yet white writing/ won't stop writing me' – 'My Meter is Percussive', Thomas Sayers Ellis

'Perhaps it is something like how old schoolers would say you heal from a snakebite: having to spit out the venom again and again until there is no more' – Saul Williams

In closing I should say that the italicised phrases in 'The N Word' come from the song 'Get Dark' by Mz Bratt (a staggering illustration of the 'colour complex' that informs our racial classifications).

JOHN CLEGG was born in 1986. His first collection, *Antler*, was published by Salt in 2012. He is currently in the final stages of a PhD at Durham University. His poems have been featured in *The Salt Book of Younger Poets* and *Best British Poetry 2012*. He writes as follows: 'The poem is set in Cairo between the wars. The figtree is not the (more familiar) Ficus Caricus but the Sycamore Fig, and the curious activity of the protagonist is an operation which may still be known colloquially as "the circumcision of the sycamore figs". Sycamore figs are one of the earliest cultivated fruit trees (perhaps the very earliest), and the practice existed long before people were aware of the rationale behind it. (The piercing mimics the action of the fig-wasp, which the fig depends on for pollination; this speeds up the ripening process of the fruit.) The fruit is quite a bit smaller than the figs we're used to in the UK, midway between a grape and a lychee. It would take a good number to make up a reasonable breakfast. A while after I'd finished the poem, I tried one, to check, and I should say that as far as I'm concerned my protagonist overstates their merits quite a bit.'

DAVID CONSTANTINE, born 1944 in Salford, Lancashire, was for thirty years a university teacher of German language and literature. He has published several volumes of poetry, most recently – 2009 – *Nine Fathom Deep*; also a novel, *Davies* (1985); and four collections of short stories, the latest being *Tea at the Midland* (2012). He is an editor and translator of Hölderlin, Goethe, Kleist and Brecht. He was the winner of 2010 BBC National Short Story Award. With his wife Helen he edited *Modern Poetry in Translation*, 2003-12. He comments: 'This is the first of a sequence of six poems written shortly before and soon after the death of a close friend. In 'Foxes, rain', and in the other poems too, I found that real local details entered my thinking about him, and became images when I tried to write about him. The tone of voice here is flat. It lifts somewhat, and briefly, into a quicker rhythm, at line 4. The chief poetic resource is lineation: how lines end, break, run over. I don't aim at it, but I'm pleased, when a poem is done, if in at least one of its lines I have managed to say what I mean in words of one syllable, as here in the last.'

EMILY CRITCHLEY holds a PhD in contemporary American women's poetry and philosophy from the University of Cambridge. She is the author of several poetry chapbooks. Her *Selected Writing: Love / All That / & OK* was published by Penned in the Margins in 2011. In 2004 she won the John Kinsella – Tracy Ryan prize for poetry and in 2011 was joint winner of the Jane Martin Prize for Poetry. She teaches English and Creative Writing at the University of Greenwich, London. She notes, 'This is the second half of a serial poem written partly in response to a poem by Joan Retallack: *Memnoir*, Hegel's *Phenomenology of Spirit* and Peter Zinovieff's libretto for *The Mask of Orpheus*, a Harrison Bertwistle opera based on the myth of Orpheus, the god of poetry, and his wife Euridice. My poem is also partly a response to the London Riots of 2011 and wonders about wider questions of morality and conscience within a society.'

FRANCINE ELENA was born in 1986 in Canterbury and grew up in London, Portugal and Scotland, graduating from the University of Edinburgh with an MA in Classics. She works in publishing as an assistant editor. 'Ode to a 1980s Baton Twirling World Champion' was the first poem she submitted for publication. Her poems have since appeared or are forthcoming in *3AM Magazine, Clinic, Poems in Which* and *The London Literary Project*. She writes: 'The inspiration for my poem started with a YouTube video of twelve-year-old Canadian Stacy Singer winning the 1989 Baton Twirling World Championship in Lausanne, Switzerland. It is a truly startling performance; I had never seen anything like it. There is an almost supernatural quality in what she is able to do that matches any world-class athlete, yet baton twirling (competitively, a kind of hyperactive freestyle gymnastics) is not recognised as an Olympic sport nor given much mainstream attention.

You can hear a crowd cheering in the video, as Singer rapidly shape-shifts through her set, but the stadium around her is eerily, and rather sadly, empty. I thought the sport (which originated from knife, torch and rifle throwing before it was adopted by little girls) deserved some recognition.

I chose the structure of a classical ode not only because it is the traditional form for praise and glorification, with its roots in Ancient Greek music and dance, but because, like baton twirling, it is a highly disciplined and rather unfashionable exercise that allows you to show off.'

CLAIRE CROWTHER has published three pamphlets and two full collections of poetry, the first of which, *Stretch of Closures*, was shortlisted for the Aldeburgh prize. Her poems and reviews have been published widely in journals such as *London Review of Books, Poetry Review, Poetry Wales, Times Literary Supplement*.

The poem describes a competition which I attended in Italy where business ideas were judged and the winners funded. The competition took place in a wood-panelled room with a Baroque painted ceiling. I see ideas as creaturely and organic so I wrote this poem to give an idea its own voice. Ideas obviously relate to humans and this one (not a winner) empathised with the woman whose idea was a winner but, of course, was taken from her to be developed.

Given the social constraint of the idea and given the history which attended the presentation of those ideas that night, I felt a sonnet was appropriate. Further, the poem demanded to be in syllabics, a favourite form of mine, because syllabics highlight, represent even, meaningless control in my view. The variety of contemporary syllabic poetry I use (similar to Marianne Moore's number-patterned lines) could be called linear nonsense. This is not a bad thing. A syllabically-counted line questions the establishment value of both free verse and metre. It also allows lineation for lineation's sake; the idea-subject of my poem is longing for just that escape from application which was denied the winners of the competition.

I write nonsense poems from time to time. It's a genre I find congenial and representative of our time if not practised much in current British poetry. While this may not be a conventional nonsense poem, it draws on the nonsense tradition. Presenting a protagonist as human who cannot exist in full human terms is a nonsense convention.

MENNA ELFYN has written over twenty books, mainly poetry, ranging from *Aderyn Bach Mewn Llaw* (1990), winner of a Welsh Arts Council Prize to Perffaith Nam/Perfect Blemish (Bloodaxe, 2005), children's novels and educational books, numerous stage, radio and television plays, and libretti, including Garden of Light for the New York Philharmonic (1999), and she co-edited the *Bloodaxe Book of Modern Welsh Poetry*. Director of the Creative Writing programme at Trinity University Carmarthen, she has received a Creative Arts Award (2008) and the International Anima Istranza Prize in Sardinia (2009). Her most recent collection is *Murmur* (Bloodaxe, 2012) a PBS Recommended Translation. She writes: 'My daughter's friend's father died and she wanted to be at the crematorium to support her. But her own daughter Beca was only three months old and there was no way she could attend alone, as she was breastfeeding. So she had to have me in tow. In a way the poem's a lullaby – isn't that what women have done throughout the ages? – sing to and soothe their babies – so it begins in a very quiet way and the voice isn't quite sure where she's going. This is how I write, believing like Wislawa Szymborska so much in the "I don't know".

I very much love the terza rima: it's the kind of form that ebbs and flows, interlocks and breaks free too. Of course in the Welsh there are far more rhymes or slant rhymes but I think this translation by Elin ap Hywel has improvised beautifully by getting alliteration and rhyme within lines to make up for end-rhymes such as "each rattle-shake a shock" which compensates for the loss of the cynghanedd in a line like "pob rhuglyn yn syn o'i siglo": not only is there rhyme but the last word has to alliterate with the last rhyme. I tend to use cynghanedd very loosely, as an underlay, as I love open form. The Welsh is musical and the language I've used is almost biblical: "eil i alar", an aisle to grief; "mintai ddwys", which Elin has turned into "grave company". I think she's mirrored the Welsh perfectly here.

Sitting in the car, I made a note that all I could see were little mounds of moles. That note was in fact the kernel of the poem: it's what gave it that extra dimension. I returned home and after a day or two read everything I could on moles. Honestly, I could have written a whole book of poems on them. And this is what one must do to get a poem right. I finally saw the paradox. Moles rebreathe – and live for a long time – so unlike us mortals. So now, it turned from a lullaby one moment, to an elegy about humankind in a way and that propelled the poem, gave it meaning.'

LEONTIA FLYNN was born in County Down in 1974. She is author of three books of poetry *These Days* (2004), *Drives* (2008) and *Profit and Loss* (2011), which was Poetry Book Society Choice for Autumn 2011, and shortlisted for the T. S. Eliot Prize. She has won the Forward Prize for first collection, the Rooney Prize for Irish literature and was this year awarded the 17th annual Lawrence O'Shaughnessy Award for Poetry of the University of St. Thomas Center for Irish Studies. She comments as follows: '"MacNeice's Mother" is written partly in response to Mac-Neice's 'Autobiography', which also contains the lines "my mother wore a yellow dress", and "the dark was talking to the dead". MacNeice's poem centres on the loss of the poet's mother at the age of five, when she suffered a breakdown and was committed to a nursing home, where she later died of tuberculosis. MacNeice's poems often feature various kinds of hauntings, suggesting that the loss of his mother affected him throughout his life and was formative to his development as a poet. I tried to suggest the importance of the woman herself, and not just her loss to the poet'

CHARLOTTE GEATER lives in London, is studying part-time for an MA at the University of Kent and works in publishing. She has previously been published in *Stop Sharpening Your Knives (3) & (4)*, *The Salt Book of Younger Poets*, and *The Rialto*. She writes: 'I wanted very much to write a poem for Pussy Riot, but I was wary of the motives that were driving me (and others) to write poems for Pussy Riot. What does it mean to say 'we are all Pussy Riot' anyway? The trial is not ours and we should not try to make it so. But we should listen to what is said from it, through it and about it.

This poem is made up of my own writing and cut up pieces of found text (from a lot of different sources). In here are comments on newspaper articles, quotations taken from TV news anchors, the bible, Pussy Riot quoting the 'hail Mary' prayer, the LRB blog (slightly mangled) and probably some other things that I have forgotten.

In the end, I wanted to write about the responses to Pussy Riot that I was seeing, especially from the liberal left, which wanted to take their art and actions as an instigation for liberal change within western socie-ties (where had they been if they thought we needed any kind of outside instigator? How can it only just have become the right time to be angry?). This was a liberal left that wanted to sell tickets to Pussy Riot concerts; a liberal left that wanted to position Pussy Riot as 'non-violent'; a liberal left that saw Pussy Riot as another commodity or brand to be exploited as long as it seemed fun and exciting. A liberal left that wasn't really listening or reading hard enough. As I write this, Masha is on hunger strike – she wasn't allowed to attend her own parole hearing. Nadya and Masha have both been denied parole. I didn't quote Pussy Riot themselves because they have already spoken and should be heard on their own terms . . . 'this freedom goes on living with every person who is not indifferent, who hears us in this country. with everyone who found shards of the trial in themselves . . .' (Masha Alyokhina)

DAI GEORGE is a poet from Cardiff, now living in London. His work has been published in the *Salt Book of Younger Poets* and *Best British Poetry 2011*. His first collection, *The Claims Office*, comes out from Seren in October. He commments: "Seven Rounds with Bill's Ghost' took a long time to write. I've touched on its genesis in an essay called 'A Fraught Inheritance' written for the edition of Poetry Wales in which the poem first appeared. The short version of the story is that it's about my grandfather, a figure that I'd always wanted to write about. Early versions of the poem were straightforward and laudatory. They received broadly encouraging but reserved feedback; it took Nick Laird, a teacher of mine at Columbia University, to say that you just can't write like that about family members after Don Paterson's 'An Elliptical Stylus'. I read the Paterson poem and took Nick's point. The choice seemed to be: give up on the poem, or rewrite it in a more combative mode. I decided to have a go at the latter, realising that the poem's central theme of boxing gave me an angle to do that. And I saw that my feelings were much more complicated than I'd thought. Bill (for that was how I came to address him) died when I was five. I felt I knew him but I didn't. All I knew were the fond, almost mythic tributes that older members of my family gave him. I wanted to prod at him, and the frustrations and privations that he must have experienced as someone growing up on the South Wales coal field of the early twentieth century, to see if a more complicated – and angry – person might respond to my provocations.'

MATTHEW GREGORY was born in Suffolk, 1984, and studied at the Norwich School of Art & Design and Goldsmiths College, where he is researching a PhD. His poems have appeared in national publications and anthologies since 2005, including the London Review of Books, Poetry London, Poetry Review and Salt's *The Best British Poetry 2011* and Bloodaxe's *Dear World & Everyone In It*. His work has been aired on BBC radio. In 2010, he received an Eric Gregory award.

He comments: 'The poem belongs to a sequence that details a series of rooms, either imagined or historical. In their entirety, the poems come together as a kind of edifice, a "house" of poems. They seem to be related to each other through particular shades – of solitariness, disintegration, a generally fuliginous kind of light – as if a certain sort of lens had been used to give a tint to each. I was living in Naples when I started work on these, and most days experienced a city and region, that from a conservative Occidental estimation of a "thriving civilisation", was a kind of living ruin. This touched the sequence, in its timbre and shape, certainly.

Here the Italian actor Marcello Mastroianni (*La Dolce Vita*, *8½*) – who I've always thought personified a very old and lonely world-weariness – appears as a kind of apparition to the Taiwanese girl, who pursues the image, or romance, of him through the internet's floating passages and recesses. This particular poem, outside of its place in my sequence, brings me to thoughts of the superconnected world's exchange of symbols and the subtle alterations in the "value" of those symbols as they travel. On the internet those isolate signs are adrift, vestiges that wash up far from home: Mastroianni and Anita Ekberg at the Fontana di Trevi as elegiac tableau of the West.'

PHILIP GROSS's *The Water Table* won the T.S. Eliot Prize in 2009, *I Spy Pinhole Eye* Wales Book of The Year 2010, and *Off Road To Everywhere* the CLPE Award for Children's Poetry 2011. *Deep Field* deals with voice and language, explored through his father's aphasia, and a new collection, *Later,* come from Bloodaxe in Autumn 2013. He has published ten novels for young people, has collaborated with artists, musicians and dancers, and since 2004 has been Professor of Creative Writing at the University of South Wales, where he leads the MPhil/PhD in Writing.

He writes: 'In the photograph a beaten-up armchair lies on its side. From the metallic look of the bare floor, where some daylight gets in through the buckled-open door, we can guess that the place is industrial. There are struts of abandoned machines. I can't go closer to see, because this is one of a set of photographs by Stephanie Gibson; I have them in a 'boxed set' called The Absent Photographer. All are of abandoned buildings, but somewhere in each you might just spot a tripod, as if even the photographer had absconded, leaving absence there to photograph itself.

None of this is in the poem . . . except the absence. The poem won't explain the photograph, or vice versa. Rather, the frame of the photograph opened into somewhere else, like that grey door swinging into what might have been somebody's private bolthole where he'd dragged in an old armchair to put his feet up between shifts . . . except it, that particular place, wasn't there. I did note, aha, the location: the Schenuit Rubber Factory, Baltimore, MD. I'm not ashamed to say that the lost words (lost but hanging in brackets, like things caught in cobwebs) came from an Internet skitter round the world's random wiki knowledge of the rubber industry. That's part of the pathos, how someone's heart– and hand-felt knowledge passes into everyone's-and-no-one's limbo. Nearby, though, and equally unseen, was the centre of gravity around which so many of my poems of the last few years have circled: my father's old age, and his loss of language and of bearings through his deep aphasia. He never worked in a Baltimore tyre factory, but maybe it's him who'd just stepped outside from that empty room, leaving such a haunted absence in the air.

DAVID HARSENT has published ten collections of poetry. The most recent, *Night* was Poetry Book Society Choice for Spring 2011 and won the Griffin International Poetry Prize, as well as being shortlisted for the Forward Prize (Best Collection), the T.S. Eliot Prize, and the Costa Poetry Prize. He is Professor of Creative Writing at the University of Roehampton and a Fellow of the Royal Society of Literature.

He comments: 'On the night before her brother's wedding, Dorothy Wordsworth went to bed wearing the ring with which William would marry Mary Hutchinson. An account of this in her journal was later heavily deleted. There has been a good deal of speculation about the deleted lines, much of it suggesting (some might say confirming) an incestuous relationship between the Wordsworths. It's certainly true that there are entries in the Grasmere Journal, not least that written on the morning of Wordsworth's marriage and containing the effaced passage, that describe an unusually passionate attachment between brother and sister. Dorothy's reaction to her brother's marriage was, if not hysterical, something close to that. And she chose to record it. So we might ask why the fact that she had worn, all night, the ring that would bind Wordsworth to another, that he came to her bedroom, took the ring from her finger, then slipped it back on and blessed her, why the account of that moment alone, in a record of distress, lay under the heavy scoring of her pen. It might be, perhaps, that betrayal is sometimes collusive. Or it might be that the pen was not Dorothy's.'

STUART HENSON received an Eric Gregory Award in 1979. Since then his work has appeared widely in journals and magazines in Britain and the US. His first two collections, *The Impossible Jigsaw* and *Ember Music*, were published by Peterloo Poets. *A Place Apart* (2004) and *The Odin Stone* (2010) are published by Shoestring Press. He comments as follows:

"The Builder' is closely based on a prose-poem 'Le Maçon', by the nine-teenth century French writer Louis 'Aloysius' Bertrand. Bertrand's gothic *fantaisies* were admired by Mallarmé and Baudelaire, who did much to promote his reputation following his early death in 1841, and his only collection, *Gaspard de la Nuit*, is a treasure-trove of dark portraits and swirling images, many cast back into the world of medieval Paris – or Bertrand's home town of Dijon. This version retains the structure and image patterns of the original but moves it in time and place. The stand-off between peace and violence that seems to shadow most of the stanza-paragraphs, and the sudden disturbing focus on the village '*incendié par des gens de guerre*' at the end of Bertrand's poem, suggested a contemporary relevance, and, sadly, an eerie sense of historical repetition.'

WAYNE HOLLOWAY-SMITH was born in Wiltshire. His debut pock-etbook, *Beloved, in case you've been wondering*, was published by Donut Press in 2011. His work has appeared or is forthcoming in *City State: New London Poetry*, *Magma*, *Erotic Review*, *The Wolf*, *New Writing*, *Stop Sharpening Your Knives 5*, *Lung Jazz: Young British Poets for Oxfam*. He lives in London and is currently working towards a PhD in English at Brunel University. He writes, 'This poem was written in response to a commission from Amy Key. Her occasional journal sets perimeters within which the poems featured are to be made. That the title should suggest 'This is a poem in which such and such happens' caught my attention in so far as the poet is forced to acknowledge that what is being created is a work of fiction. The potential for removal of immediacy. The potential for removal of the imperative voice of the poet. The potential for removal of an illusion of reality. It seems to me that the poet and reader have an opportunity in all of this to strike up a novel kind of agreement. The poet may take the invitation to perform these things and – fingers-crossed – make something good/ fun/ interesting appear on the page, the reader all the while enjoying the spectacle. I may be completely mistaken.'

SARAH HOWE was born in Hong Kong in 1983. Her tall-lighthouse pamphlet, *A Certain Chinese Encyclopedia*, won an Eric Gregory Award in 2010. Her work appears in *The Salt Book of Younger Poets* (2011) and *Dear World & Everyone In It* (Bloodaxe, 2013). In 2012-13, she is the holder of the Harper-Wood Studentship for poetry from St John's College, Cambridge. Her first collection is forthcoming from Chatto in 2015.

She writes: 'There was a while after university when I thought I might become a painter. I had a scholarship from my former college which granted me a year to do nothing but paint. I worked through the night in an oil-splattered, fume-heady studio above a furniture shop in Cambridge. In summer 2010, I began to write a poem called 'A painting' which looked back on that time. Rather than the act of painting itself, the most vivid and pleasurable details that returned to me were the manual, doggedly material tasks that supported it. Planting staples into pine and canvas, scraping a barnacled palette, teasing stiffened brushes back to life in the sink. The turpentine jar first turned up in the middle of that poem's catalogue of studio paraphernalia. But with each draft the jar's description became more elaborate, more fascinated, and more phenomenological, until it outgrew its space in the parent poem. Snipped out, that cutting became 'Scrying: turpentine'. Now the two poems sit together like a diptych.

Partway through my painting year I got more finicky about materials and stretched to more expensive paints. When it came to cutting the fatty richness of those glorious pigments, I couldn't keep using the same miserly white spirit meant for cleaning brushes, but switched to the highest-grade turpentine I could afford. Spoiled by light, it came in silver canisters a little smaller than a cocktail shaker. Because of the turpentine's cost, I followed a daily ritual which employed two jars. One jam jar was the working vessel, for dipping brushes in. At work's end I would decant its clouded, mineraly liquid into another storage jar. Over many hours the paint particles would sediment into a grey-brown sludge, leaving the turpentine clear and usable once more, though irreversibly tinted with that particular canvas's dominant note. In the poem the two jars have become one, as would happen on the odd day when I forgot to do the pouring.'

A.B. JACKSON's first book, *Fire Stations*, was published by Anvil Press in 2003 and won the Forward Prize for Best First Collection that year. In 2010 he won first prize in the Edwin Morgan International Poetry Competition, and in 2011 Donut Press published a limited edition pamphlet, *Apocrypha*, which was the Poetry Book Society's Pamphlet Choice for Summer 2011. His poems have appeared in the TLS, The Guardian, Poetry Review, The Dark Horse, and Magma. He is currently studying for a PhD in Creative Writing at Sheffield Hallam University on the subject of polar exploration and contemporary poetry.

He comments: 'In December 2009 I came across Philemon Holland's 1601 translation of Pliny the Elder's *Natural History*, composed in the first century AD. This Roman encyclopedia contained vital information about unicorns and Hippocentaurs alongside lunar observations and the price of Myrrh, while the Holland translation added a further gloss of Elizabethan language and interpretation. The sequence I went on to write, "Natural History", is an equal mix of Holland's text and my own. The original spelling was mostly retained with only a few exceptions: "bloud" was modernised to "blood", for example, in order to avoid ambiguities in pronunciation as the eye fell on the unfamiliar. My original additions followed these spelling conventions and – in the spirit of discovery – I felt free to include made-up words. For the most part I hope the ancient and modern will look seamless; on occasion, however, I have deliberately added a contemporary phrase in order to highlight the intertextual playfulness of the project. For those interested in the source material, the poems were constructed from book VIII of *Natural History*, concerning land creatures. The work took place in Velvet Elvis on Dumbarton Road, Glasgow, with the aid of Guinness.'

ANDREW JAMISON was born in Northern Ireland in 1986. His first collection, *Happy Hour*, was published by Gallery Press in 2012. He teaches English at Bristol Grammar School. He writes, 'To ask what a poem is about, in many ways, is to ask where a poem has come from. This poem of mine comes from the following places: Horsforth, Yorkshire, May 2012, the stolen moment of a solitary weekday evening, the beginning of summer. I lived in Yorkshire for two years, training to be an English teacher. I soon came to realise that May, as well as ushering in the northern English summer, was also a time when many of my students started to peel off on study leave for their exams, meaning I had more time to myself in the days and evenings to read, write or go for a walk. Teacher training can be a fairly tumultuous affair, and when I wrote this poem I was in the final stages of it and knew that soon I'd be leaving Yorkshire for Bristol, and that *Happy Hour*, my first collection, would be published in July. So, I would say there is a sense of an ending in this poem, a sense of a dénouement, as well as a sense of summer and new paths opening up.'

ALAN JENKINS is Deputy Editor and Poetry Editor at the *TLS*, and has taught creative writing in the USA, London and Paris. His books of poetry include *The Drift* (2000), *A Shorter Life* (2005) and *Revenants* (2013); *Drunken Boats*, containing his acclaimed translation of Rimbaud's 'Le Bateau ivre', was published in 2007, and *Blue Days (The Sailor's Return)* in 2010. *A Short History of Snakes*, selected poems, was published in 2001 by Grove Press, New York. He is a Fellow of the Royal Society of Literature. He comments, 'I'm pretty sure each of us, whatever our actual situation, harbours a fantasy of escape – into the other life, the otherwhere . Mine is a harbour, in fact – or it starts in one, and involves a boat, a voyage by sea. I must have picked this up more or less unconsciously from my father, who loved boats, but fleshed out his dream from novels he also loved (which I read and loved in my turn), by Joseph Conrad and Georges Simenon. 'Sea Music' isn't the first poem of mine to draw on all this – though it draws on odds and ends of poetry, too: Wallace Stevens is there, as are (vestigially) Ezra Pound and Louis MacNeice. But they're not the point, so it wouldn't matter in the least if no one noticed them. Phrases of theirs are just part of the speaker's daydream, which like any daydream contains elements of memory, both blissful and painful, generalized and (very) specific. The siren-voices offer him rather different versions of himself – harsher but not, by the end, wholly unforgiving. (Which is another dream, of course: the dream of forgiveness.) The palm has gone now, but it was there, once – like one I also saw on a metro station in – was it Barcelona?'

CHRIS MCCABE's collections are *The Hutton Inquiry, Zeppelins* and *THE RESTRUCTURE* (all with Salt). His work has been described by *The Guardian* as 'an impressively inventive survey of the uses of English in the early 21st century'. He has recorded a CD with the Poetry Archive and has had work included in numerous anthologies. His plays *Shud Thames, Broken Wharf* (published by Penned in the Margins as a limited edition box) and *Mudflats* have been performed in London and Liverpool. He works as the Poetry Librarian at The Saison Poetry Library and teaches for The Poetry School. He writes, '*The Alchemist* is one of a sequence of nine poems about Jacobean drama, each of which has the title of a specific play. Each poem is spoken through the voice of a spurned or aspiring lover and is set at the point of the play's first London performance, at the location of that playhouse. I took the notion of imagining the original players dragging their character roles onto the streets and playing out the emotions for real, for themselves, forgetting that their words are supposed to be a theatrical conceit. I also experimented with anachronistic language, that is : I gave the characters free-reign to plunder the current vernacular of late capitalism and to use that language as a way to illustrate their various disillusionments and anger. This anachronism works in reverse too, allowing me to mine the often cryptic and compressed pre-dictionary language of the poet-playwrights to explore the emotional | factual | political backdrop of being in the world in 2012. I often introduce *The Alchemist* at readings as a poem about commuting. Alchemy seemed like a useful way of thinking about that transformation of the self through a long commute into London. In form the poems are prose sonnets written in sprung rhythm.'

JOHN MCCULLOUGH's first collection *The Frost Fairs* (Salt) won the Polari First Book Prize for 2012 and was a Book of the Year for *The Independent* and The Poetry School. He lives in Hove and teaches creative writing for the Open University and New Writing South. He comments, 'Exclamation marks are generally discouraged in literary writing. Style guides and course books routinely point out how outside dialogue they can undermine subtlety, introducing a humorous excess of feeling which feels a little too close to shouting. A glorious exception is Frank O'Hara's poetry which hosts a giddy forest of these flabbergasted symbols known variously as screamers, gaspers, startlers and, by less polite subeditors, as dogs' cocks.

No one's sure exactly when the first exclamation mark was used though it's often speculated that its origins lie in Latin, and specifically the vertical representation of the word *io*, or joy. I wanted to imagine that on its early travels across medieval England that it carried something of the distasteful, risqué aspects which still follow it (or *dog* it) today. I researched the writing implements of the time and decided that I wanted the form of the poem to echo the shape of an exclamation mark in some way, hence the choice of a long pillar of text with the last four lines in italics to evoke the point. That sense of a screamer representing the unsayable, a degree of emotion for which language is inadequate, I hope is also present in the wordless title.'

PATRICK McGUINNESS is the author of two books of poetry, *The Canals of Mars* (2004) and *Jilted City* (2010), and a novel, *The Last Hundred Days* (2010). His next book, *Other People's Countries*, appears in 2014 from Cape. He teaches French at Oxford University. He comments, 'The poems that Best British Poetry's editors choose of mine all seem to be about death or Belgium; or, as here, both. The recurrence of these two universals in my work is certainly noticeable, but I have occasionally written about other things – memory, childhood, travel and also the Great Indoors. This poem touches on all of these, and is about my grandmother, who was a dressmaker in a small Walloon town on the French/Belgian border where I was brought up. It's about her work and her presence when I was small and Belgian, and about her aura now that I'm middle aged and English. I kept the Stockmann mannequins, which still have the same effect on me.'

EDWARD MACKAY studied History and English at Oxford University and lives in east London where he has worked in mediation, community development and creative writing. His poetry was shortlisted for the inaugural Picador Poetry Prize (2011), commended in the Emerge Escalator competition (2010) and shortlisted for an Eric Gregory Award (2009). He has been widely published in magazines and anthologies. His debut chapbook, *Swarming* is available from Salt.

He writes, '*Afterword* is part of an elegiac series sharing title, form and theme, distinguished by dedicatee. Tsutomu Yamaguchi (1916 – 2010) was the only *hibakusha* (bomb-affected person) to survive both US atomic attacks on Japan. Yamaguchi returned home to Nagasaki after being injured on a business trip to Hiroshima. Each *Afterword* is "for" a real figure who participated in a historically significant moment, purposefully blurring history's drivers with the contingently involved. Each dedicatee lived a long "ordinary" life after a moment of fame or notoriety. Another *Afterword* finds George Loveless, one of the so-called Tolpuddle Martyrs, in Canada during his second (self-imposed) exile after returning from transportation to Australia, disquieted by fame and disillusioned with "home". Another takes Peter Chappell, who led the chaotic, eccentric, inspiring and successful campaign to release George Davis, wrongfully convicted in 1975 for armed robbery (only to see Davis later return to prison for a robbery he *did* commit). Each is a "ripple" poem, a form created by Roddy Lumsden (adapting the anagrammatic poetry of Terrance Hayes) taking the consonants of a word associated with the dedicatee (here *atomic*; for Chappell, *innocent*; and for Loveless, *martyr*) and concluding each line with a word which employs only these sounds, plus vowels (in any order) – a poetic cousin of Muldoon's "fuzzy rhyme". In *Afterwords*, the word-choices and their 'rippling' reconfiguration acknowledge the association and problematise the supposed significance, in the long afteryears, of the fleeting events through which the dedicatees have been understood.

The ongoing project of the *Afterword* poems is to inhabit the shadow of nominally pivotal moments in semi-public lives and speculatively engage with the disappointments, confusions, choices and compromises – as well as hopes – that might be found at the borders of these totems. In addition to being published in *Shearsman*, Yamaguchi's *Afterword* was one of 300 poems from poets around the world dropped in a poetry "bombing" of London by artists' collective Casagrande as part of *Poetry Parnassus* festival in 2012.'

ANDREW MCMILLAN was born in 1988. His poetry is collected in three pamphlets, most recently *the moon is a supporting player* (2011) and *protest of the physical* (2013) both from Red Squirrel Press. His commission for the 2012 Yorkshire Cultural Olympiad was featured on Radio 4's *Today* programme. In 2012 he was named as a 'New Voice' by both Aldeburgh Poetry Festival and Latitude Festival. He lectures in Creative Writing at Liverpool John Moores University and is currently working on a first collection.

He comments, 'ABBA were on the television. Someone commented how, after their sudden rise to fame after winning the Eurovision, the band were touring songs that weren't actually in their first language. That interested me and was the start of the poem; although it ends up set in an unnamed era and area that maybe has the rural parts of Eastern Europe in mind. It became, for me, about what gets missed between people, transience, about what goes unsaid. Formally, I feel that breath spaces, rather than punctuation, offers a more natural speech pattern to a poem and I'm interested in what happens when words ("lonelyhaircut cellist") are pushed together to create new ones. The title, which makes an appearance in the last line, is the title of an ABBA song from their sixth studio album. Steffan is the name of a previous partner who is in the background of the poem; his name also has the added quality of scanning well in a line which needed a two-syllable name – it is nice when the departed retain some use to us. Maybe it is also ("foreign voice", "barely understand the lines") somewhat about the life and process of a poet as well. Maybe not. It was written on a Christmas stay at my parents' house, returning to which always has the twin heimlich/unheimlich feel. Maybe that is in the background here too. Maybe not. The "precious bird" line is about as self-consciously poetic as I've ever allowed myself to get. It would have been too loud an ending and a quieter, plainer line was needed to finish on. Reading the poem back I see there are a lot of ands being used; I'm sorry about that. And maybe I'm not.'

KONA MACPHEE grew up in Australia and now lives in Perthshire, where she works as a freelance media producer and runs the Muse Tuners creative mentoring agency. She received an Eric Gregory Award in 1998 and her first collection, *Tails*, was published by Bloodaxe Books in 2004. Her second Bloodaxe collection, *Perfect Blue*, was awarded the Geoffrey Faber Memorial Prize for 2010. Her third collection, *What Long Miles* was published by Bloodaxe in March 2013. She writes the following, 'I always liked the content of this poem, but was never happy with the title (which went through a number of equally unsatisfactory incarnations). Principally for this reason, I didn't include it in my latest collection *What Long Miles*. The poem's inspiration is the animal origin (in evolutionary terms) of our own brains/minds, and the legacy that we might carry as a result – particularly in terms of our 'irrational' emotional reactions and endocrine responses.'

ALLISON MCVETY's *The Night Trotsky Came to Stay* (Smith|Doorstop) was shortlisted for the Forward Best First Collection Prize. Allison's poems have appeared in *Poetry London, Poetry Review, Guardian, Times*, have been broadcast on BBC radio and have appeared in *Forward Poems of the Decade 2002–2011*. A second collection, *Miming Happiness* was published in 2010 and in 2011 she won the National Poetry Competition. She writes, 'In the poem, packed as it is with the paraphernalia of living, I wanted to explore that briefest of moments when disbelief in the fact of an event – in this instance the death of a wife – can overcome its reality; when an emotion as fantastical as love might just be powerful enough to reverse events and revive her. Although the poem – which is comprised of a single sentence and column in order to echo the musical shape of the symphonic poem – concerns itself with the aftermath of a still and quiet death, I wanted it to begin with sound: that loud and turbulent opening of Sibelius' deeply nationalist tone poem, *Finlandia*. This is not simply because it was a favourite symphony of my dad's but also because it moves from manic percussion to poem and finally to prayer; swelling from outrage to love, to that last, almost silent, breath.'

D.S. MARRIOTT's latest collection of poetry is *The Bloods* (Shearsman Books, 2011). His work has appeared in *Out of Bounds: British black & Asian Poets*, ed Jackie Kay (Bloodaxe Books, 2012) and *Identity Parade: New British and Irish Poets*, ed. Roddy Lumsden (Bloodaxe Books, 2010). He is currently working on a new manuscript, called *In Neuter*. He comments, '"The Redeemers" is the first poem of my new collection, *In Neuter*, which I am currently writing. It continues my interest in the evasive clarities (so to speak) of prose, and the untidy intimacies of a black demotic, the sounds and music of its speech. I'd like to think that this is where the balance and equilibrium of the poem meets language staggering homewards on its feet. The poem itself is a kind of perverse hymnal to the waste and trash of the world, how they/it is produced, recycled, and endlessly produced as the abject littoral of our fast-paced ephemeral culture, and, last but not least, how language itself is also a kind of dance and a meditation of the meaning of such ephemera, of their splendour and awful brevity.'

GLYN MAXWELL's books of poetry include *The Nerve, The Sugar Mile, One Thousand Nights and Counting: Selected Poems,* and *Pluto*. He has won the Geoffrey Faber Memorial Prize and the E.M.Forster Prize from the American Academy, and been shortlisted many times for the T.S.Eliot, Forward or Whitbread/Costa Prizes. His critical guide *On Poetry* was published in 2012. His plays include *The Lifeblood* (British Theatre Guide's 'Best Play' on the Edinburgh Fringe, 2004) and *Liberty*, which premiered at Shakespeare's Globe in 2008. He lectures in Creative Writing at the University of Essex.

He comments, '"Christmas Seven Times Seven" was written on Christmas morning, 2010. I made a conscious decision to see what it would be like to begin a day that had always begun loudly, joyfully, nostalgically, sentimentally around the hearths of various loved ones – quite alone in my flat in London. So I put off the traditional appearance north of here at my parents' or south of here at my daughter's ("two whole families") until – well, until I'd done something. And the only possible reward to be reaped from this difficult exploration was a completed poem, so this is what took shape. It chimed with some other poems I'd written before and would write after it – in examining the strange no man's land between a faith held and a faith explained away. For, though I long ago lost belief in any literal truth in Christian doctrine, a strong inexplicable sense of mystery and force remains and so far in my exploration I have been able to locate the source of that power only in time itself. I mean that in the absence of what Larkin in "Aubade" called religion's "vast, moth-eaten musical brocade" I seem to have substituted – or tried to lift into place – poetic work itself. Art. That what I hear in poetry – not so much Frost's "stay against confusion" but a bid to parlay with *time itself* – carries for me the power that perhaps these mystical systems carry for believers. Well I was alone with something powerful that morning, and it was hard to be around it. I couldn't wait to be on the M25 and heading back to life.'

CHRISTOPHER MIDDLETON was born in Truro, Cornwall, in 1926. He studied at Merton College, Oxford, and then taught at the University of Zurich, at King's College, London, and finally as Professor of Germanic Languages at the University of Texas, Austin. He has published translations of Robert Walser, Nietzsche, Holderlin, Goethe, Gert Hofmann and many others. Over the last two decades Carcanet has published six books of his poems, *Intimate Chronicles* (1996), one book of his experimental prose and two volumes of essays, as well as his *Selected Writings* and *Faint Harps and Silver Voices*, a collection of verse translations.

He writes, 'I'd been acquainted with Celan's poems (even translating them) since the mid-Fifties, and during the Sixties became bemused by their increasing involution. The poem came out of the blue in 2010. Common usage requires "ghosting" to put authorship in doubt. In the poem, Celan's haunting prepossessions and tortuous mannerism have become (as it were) authors of him. He is the (unstated) fugitive being tracked by the men among the trees. The crystal (unstained) of his word, to be breathed at all, finally dissolves us in music. But these are only gists and there had to be details. This poem is to appear in *Forty Days in the Calypso Saloon* (The Sheep Meadow Press, USA, 2013) and afresh in *Collected Later Poems* (Carcanet Press, 2014).'

KATE MILLER lives and works in London, a graduate of Cambridge and London Universities. An artist and teacher for thirty years, she has been writing for ten. Her first collection *The Observances* will be published in 2015. She comments, 'Although first published in 2012 the drafts of "Salvage" go back to March 2006 when I was a Masters student with Jo Shapcott. She elicited a run of water poems to which it became the coda, or so it says on one draft. After dividing it from the mother poem that Jo had called "a lively animal of water" (its subject water sources), this stayed small at twelve lines long, falling naturally into tercets. Eighty per cent remained unchanged but things that the flood carried altered: a wheelbarrow and even washed-up toys are pencilled over some versions. One of many farmland poems, it muddles up experiences from different geographies as dreams do. Cows wrestling for precedence in a stone walled lane in Portugal have fused with ruinous floods on the Rother in Sussex and the Ouvèze in the Vaucluse. Clouds and domesticated birds, I realise, are recurrent in my work but I have only slowly recognised how often I rearrange and isolate aspects of a scantily inhabited landscape, as the artist Miró did with his family farm, in a metaphorical way. This poem did not strictly have a long gestation but it took five years to mature.'

HELEN MORT was born in Sheffield in 1985. She has published two chapbooks with tall-lighthouse press, *the shape of every box* and *a pint for the ghost* and her pamphlet *Lie of the Land* was written while Poet in Residence at The Wordsworth Trust, Grasmere. Helen's first full collection *Division Street* is forthcoming from Chatto & Windus. She comments, 'This poem started life when I was walking down Shoreham Street in Sheffield: the person I was with started telling me about the historical relationship between Brazil and the United Kingdom, how there'd been a trade agreement in the 1800s which involved Brazil having to buy ice skates from the UK (along with other items useless in a hot climate). When I got home, I couldn't find out if that was true or apocryphal, but the idea of these disused ice skates wouldn't leave me alone.

Months later, I was out running through Staveley, Chesterfield – an industrial / ex industrial landscape that's about as distant from Brazil as you can imagine – and I heard the first line of the poem, quite insistently, as I ran. It seemed like a provocation. The word "admit" was really important for some reason.

The poem didn't find its form on the page until I showed an early draft to another poet who suggested the run-on title and the three line stanzas. One of the difficulties about writing while I run is that I know what it should sound like but I'm not always sure what it should look like. The suggestion of the run-on title made me re-structure and shorten the stanzas and was interesting for me because I don't normally write like that – in fact, my titles are usually self-explanatory, mundane last-minute additions to the poem. What's the addressee really being asked to admit? I don't know, and if I did, I probably wouldn't want to tell you. But, like many of the poems I end up writing, the backdrop to the idea of the ice skates in their locked room was a sense of loneliness, and one that seems unwarranted.'

ALISTAIR NOON's first full-length collection is *Earth Records* (Nine Arches, 2012), shortlisted for the 2013 Michael Murphy Memorial Prize. He has also published a dozen chapbooks of poetry and translations from German and Russian from various presses. Born in 1970, he grew up in Aylesbury and has lived in Berlin since the early nineties, where he works as a translator. He comments, 'I picked up the Marx quote somewhere I can't remember, as the only Marx I've actually read is the Manifesto. As a student I did a summer job in a pizza and flan-packing factory in my home town, night shifts. There was an all-night DJ-less radio station which was on every night without fail, with a playlist that invariably included The Eagles' *Hotel California* and The Mamas and the Papas' *California Dreamin'*. Which was appropriate, as the factory – though not actually part of it – wasn't far from the California Industrial Estate.

Not a few of my co-packers were from the North-East and Scotland, with accents unblunted enough by the South to indicate that they hadn't been there long and were there for the job. I was generally through and done after the normal eight-hour shift, but plenty of them would carry on with another two to four hours' overtime, regularly. I remember one bloke having a nap in the canteen between two shifts. You needed the best part of fifteen minutes to get changed, suited up and disinfected before actually starting work. The punch-clock was on the other side of the changing rooms. The poem is part of the 40-sonnet sequence "Earth Records", from the book of the same name. If you like poems about factories, there's another one there about a cigarette manufacturing plant.'

RICHARD O'BRIEN was a Foyle Young Poet in 2006 and 2007. His first pamphlet, *your own devices,* appeared in 2009 on tall-lighthouse press, and his work has appeared in *Poetry London, The Erotic Review,* and *The Salt Book of Younger Poets.* He has recently read at the BBC Proms, and has two pamphlets forthcoming with Dead Ink and The Emma Press. He is currently studying for an MA in Shakespeare and Creativity, and runs a blog (The Scallop Shell) dedicated to the close-reading of contemporary poetry.

He comments, '"So Much Will Waste" is by no means the only attempt I have made at rewriting John Donne's "The Flea" over the last five years, though certainly one of the most sustained. The poem dates from 2009, when I did actually attend a blood donation session at the Methodist chapel in Deeping St. James, Lincolnshire, but the more romantic/sleazy aspects of the narrative have no grounding in reality – I have never knowingly used "baby" as a spoken epithet. It was initially a much more tentative, defeatist poem, in which 'the window closes' before anyone says anything and the protagonist goes home sad and alone, miserably clutching a Tuc biscuit. The first draft was – well, quite bloodless, really. For its current form I have to thank Clare Pollard, whose suggestions for improvement on an Arvon course ("I want you to get the girl!") constituted the first, if not the last, time that I have had an editorial session turn into relationship counselling.

In terms of content, the word "blood" appears seven times in the pamphlet I have just finished editing for Dead Ink, so it would seem that I just like blood in general. I'm also fascinated by Renaissance views of how the body worked, and especially by the idea that sex and the sighs of unrequited lovers were both expenditures of energy capable of shortening lifespan. The *carpe diem* elements of the poem do have a certain grand-standing desperation to them, though perhaps it's unfair to confuse the influence of Jacobean literature with the general effects of being nineteen.'

SEAN O'BRIEN's *Collected Poems* appeared from Picador in 2012. He is the editor, with Don Paterson, of *Train Songs*, an anthology of railway poems to be published by Faber in autumn 2013. Current projects include translations, with Daniel Hahn, of the *Selected Poems* of Corsino Fortes. O'Brien is Professor of Creative Writing at Newcastle University.

RICHARD OSMOND was born in 1987. He is the co-editor of *13 Pages*, a magazine of contemporary poetry. His work has been published in The Financial Times, Magma, fuselit and n+1, among others, and anthologised in *Best British Poetry 2011*, *Birdbook II* and *The Salt Book of Younger Poets*. By day, he works as a forager for a wild food company in St Albans, collecting edible plants, fruits and fungi among the hedgerows of Hertfordshire. He writes, 'This poem was written in pastiche of Gerard Manley Hopkins (its shape, rhyme scheme and post-lapsarian themes are indebted to *The Binsey Poplars*). It was originally inspired by a series of classes on *Sound and Sense* I took as part of a Master's degree in creative writing. During these classes, a good deal of time was spent discussing the importance of subtly patterned sound in poetry.

Gerard Manley Hopkins was often put forward as an example of a poet guilty of excessive patterning. His densely alliterative, assonant and consonant lines, most agreed, tended to detract from the meaning of the words of which they were composed. It was for this reason that Don Paterson, the poet leading the classes, spoke the words now used as the poem's epigraph:

Sometimes I read Hopkins and think, "It's grand, but what did you make all that noise for? It sounds like someone throwing hammers down a well." Hopkins, of course, would beg to differ. For him, the patterning and echoing of common sounds in different words was of great, perhaps prime, importance. He was a poet on a grand mission to find, beneath the most basic phonetic elements of speech, some kind of universal and authentic real-ness and rightness in language. He sought a divine, non-arbitrary, non-imaginary link between the sounds we use and the things we mean. My poem is simply his considered, Catholic apology for doing so so noisily.'

RUTH PADEL's collections include *Darwin – A Life in Poems* and *The Mara Crossing*, a meditation on migration in birds, animals and people. She is Fellow of the Royal Society of Literature and Zoological Society of London and is Teaching Fellow in Poetry at Kings College London. Her works on reading poems include *The Poem and the Journey* and *Silent Letters of the Alphabet*, her Bloodaxe lectures on poetry's use of silence.

She writes as follows, 'The molecular biologist Reiji Okazaki was born in Hiroshima 1930 and irradiated 1945 by the atomic bomb. He died from leukemia 1975 but before that, in 1966, working with his wife, the scientist Tsuneko Okazaki, he discovered the role played during DNA replication by what are now called the Okazaki Fragments. These are the newly-synthesized morsels formed against the movement of the replication fork on the "lagging" strand of a DNA molecule, which runs in the opposite direction to the leading strand.'

REBECCA PERRY is a graduate of Manchester's Centre for New Writing and currently lives in London.

Her poetry has appeared most recently in *Poetry London*, *The Rialto* and *The Salt Anthology of New Writing*, and she placed 3rd in the 2012 Salt Prize for Best Individual Poem. Her pamphlet, *little armoured*, published by Seren in 2012, won the Poetry Wales Purple Moose Prize and was a Poetry Book Society Choice. She writes, 'I suppose I wanted this poem to take a look at the relationships we build with words throughout our lives, and how the associations we make with them inform not just how we experience those words, but how we experience the world through language. I like the idea that, from the second we hear or learn a word, we start embellishing it with our own memories, thoughts, feelings and experiences, building a sort of private secondary language that only we can access and understand. Essentially, that once we take into account the (often multiple) "true" meanings a word has, then pile on our own associations, things get a bit muddy. Of course this is nothing that hasn't been said before, but I'd always liked the idea of one day exploring that in a poem. The trigger for actually writing it came when I was looking something up in my dictionary and noticed 'inner man' – with its mean-ings ranging from "soul" to "stomach"– and then, scanning down a few words, "inner woman" (with no entry of its own) referring back up to "inner man". I was delighted by its oddness, intrigued by its origin, and annoyed by its masculine bias. I also realised I'd immediately started to layer it with my own associations (Henry VIII, a woman with a hole in her middle, Death Becomes Her . . .) after I'd read the definition. So I decided to spend a bit of time with my dictionary searching for other words that interested me, noting down my associations first, and then reading the definition afterwards.'

PASCALE PETIT's latest collection, *What the Water Gave Me: Poems after Frida Kahlo* (Seren, 2010), was shortlisted for both the T.S. Eliot prize and Wales Book of the Year, and was a book of the year in the *Observer*. Black Lawrence Press published an American edition in 2011. She has published five collections, two others of which, *The Huntress* and *The Zoo Father*, were also shortlisted for the T.S. Eliot prize. In 2004 the Poetry Book Society selected her as a Next Generation Poet. She tutors poetry courses for Tate Modern and The Poetry School.

She writes, 'The poem 'Sainte-Chapelle' is from my sixth collection, *Fauverie*, due from Seren in 2014. The book charts my rediscovery of the city of my birth, where my father lived and died. It is a follow-up to my second collection *The Zoo Father*, where I wrote about my father's reappearance after he had vanished for thirty-five years. When he made contact, he was living in the Latin Quarter, in a tiny flat, dying of emphysema. It's only now though that I have explored my hometown in depth. When I visited him in his sickbed there wasn't time, as I used to spend all afternoon and evening with him, inside a claustrophobic room. Although I lived in Paris as a child, I hadn't heard of La Sainte-Chapelle and only saw it for the first time last year. I wanted to bring the play of stained glass colours into my father's dingy room and onto his face. I trained as a sculptor and have tried blowing glass; it's a dangerous process as the heat from the furnace can be sucked into the lungs. It also requires strong lung capacity, which I don't have, and my father certainly lacked. When I stood inside the chapel, with its fifty-foot-high windows casting lozenges of light over my face and hands, I felt as if I was inside the organs of a body made of light.'

HEATHER PHILLIPSON is an artist and poet. She received an Eric Gregory Award in 2008 and a Faber New Poets Award in 2009. Her pamphlet was published by Faber and Faber in 2009; her text *NOT AN ESSAY* by Penned in the Margins in 2012; and her first book-length collection, *Instant-flex 718*, by Bloodaxe Books in 2013. As an artist, Heather Phillipson works with video, sound, sculpture and live events. She has recently exhibited at the Whitechapel Gallery, the ICA, South London Gallery, Flat Time House, Zabludowicz Collection (all London), BALTIC Centre for Contemporary Art (Gateshead) and Kunsthalle Basel (Switzerland).

She comments as follows, '"The objects should be made to look as if they want to be there" (Robert Bresson). So I review the cotton – short, startled, pained. Then ask: what's it up to? why? am I responsible/ implicated? We exist in a world in which THINGS overflow and prolifer- ate. We ought to give them parlance, dig deep into their substructures, triple-dip to their undersides. Not slope off quietly. When everything is driven by demands for growth, progress, performance, what about the mute lumps, ripped logic, the occasional pleasures of disappointment? We are drawn into a process that wears us out, submerged and segmented in all directions. But an old thing is renewed if you detach it from its sur- roundings. I think of what Cézanne said about the carrot – "The day is coming when a single carrot, freshly observed, will set off a revolution." Ditch habit and automatism, be ignorant and curious, alerted: the mind is so persuasive that what is thought might happen.'

JODY PORTER is poetry editor of socialist daily newspaper the Morning Star, and between 2004 and 2008 was editor of online poetry maga- zine zafusy. His work has appeared in *Magma*, *South Bank*, *Rising* and the *International Times*, as well as the anthologies *Catechism: Poems for Pussy Riot* and the *Robin Hood Book*. Originally from Essex, he lives in London where he's involved with running events at the Stoke New- ington Literary Festival. He comments, 'The Baader-Meinhof phenom- enon is that experience when, soon after you first become aware of some obscure piece of trivia or information, that same piece of trivia or information seems to crop up everywhere you look. Coincidences and patterns emerge where none might exist. After noticing with increasing frequency the word "black" in the names of bands, I started to maintain a list. With a few obvious exceptions (e.g. Black Lace) the bands seemed to share a common thread, and I started looking for a way to bring them together into a poem. An accidental pint in The World's End, Camden, eventually led to this one.'

KATE POTTS' poetry pamphlet *Whichever Music* (tall-lighthouse, 2008) was a Poetry Book Society Choice and was shortlisted for a Michael Marks Award. Her first full-length collection is *Pure Hustle* (Bloodaxe, 2011). Her poetry has been widely published in magazines and antholo- gies, most recently *Dear World and Everyone In It* (Bloodaxe, 2013). Kate teaches creative writing for Morley College, and is a writer in residence at Kingston University. She is working towards a PhD on radio poetry. She comments, 'I wrote *Thirty-three* in August 2011, a few weeks after the riots that erupted in cities across the UK that summer. In 2011, most of my friends (and my ex-boyfriends) seemed to have found long-term partners and were thinking about buying or renting homes for the long-term and starting families. I wasn't in the same situation, and *Thirty-three* was an exploration of my ambivalent feelings about the whole idea of "settling down." I enjoyed imagining a sort of picture-book, Truman show-esque existence for the exes in the poem, and contrasting it with the wild, dilapidated state of the poet's surroundings (the poem paints a pretty accurate picture of the garden of the flat where I lived at the time). In the end, though, the poem hangs on a tacit acknowledgement of anger and want.

I think "Thirty-three" marked a subtle shift in my writing. Its voice is less distinct from my own than the voices of most of my previous poems, and its subject matter is more explicitly personal. At the moment I'm experimenting with fictional voices as part of the radio project I'm working on, so I spend much of the writing time I have left over writing poems that are more like *Thirty-three*.

SAM RIVIERE's poems have appeared in various places including *The Guardian, AnOther Magazine, New Statesman,* and *Financial Times.* He received an Eric Gregory Award in 2009. His debut pamphlet was published by Faber in 2010, followed by *81 Austerities* in 2012, his first collection, which won the Forward Prize for Best First Collection. He writes, 'I don't think I feel very inclined to say anything about this poem, except that it is a love poem.'

MICHAEL SYMMONS ROBERTS was born in 1963 in Preston, Lancashire. His poetry has won the Whitbread Poetry Award, and been shortlisted for the Griffin International Poetry Prize, the Forward Prize, and three times for the T.S. Eliot Prize. He has received major awards from the Arts Council and the Society of Authors. His sixth collection – *Drysalter* – was published by Cape in 2013 and won the 2013 Forward Prize. He is Professor of Poetry at Manchester Metropolitan University.

He writes, 'This poem is part of *Drysalter,* a collection of 150 poems, each of 15 lines. The book takes its name from the ancient trade in powders and drugs, salts and dyes, paints and cures. But I also liked the way the word nodded to the "psalter". Medieval psalters contained both sacred and profane – the passion and despair of the Psalms, but also marginalia, jokes, myths and tall stories. Once I'd started on these 15-liners, I didn't want to write in any other form. They gave me a good sense of constraint (for the last five years I've never had to ask a poem how long it's going to be), and great freedom too – these poems could be shaped in three five-line stanzas, or five three-line stanzas, or a block of free verse, or couplets with a single last line, or seven-line stanzas with a single line between them. This particular poem is rooted in my early twenties, when I first read some George Seferis poems in translation, and one poem – *Euripides, the Athenian* – stopped me in my tracks. That line (*"The time came, and the dogs tore him to pieces"*) has been in my head ever since – the brutal beauty of it, its fatalism. In his poem, it's the last line, so I decided to make it the first line of this new poem.'

ROBIN ROBERTSON is from the north-east coast of Scotland. He has published five collections of poetry – most recently *Hill of Doors* – and received a number of accolades, including the Petrarch Prize, the E.M. Forster Award from the American Academy of Arts and Letters, the Cholmondeley Award and all three Forward Prizes. He has also edited a collection of essays, *Mortification: Writers' Stories of Their Public Shame*, translated two plays of Euripides, *Medea* and the *Bacchae*, and, in 2006, published *The Deleted World*, a selection of free English versions of poems by the Nobel laureate Tomas Tranströmer.

He writes, 'The poem is so straightforward it needs no gloss: four seasons, four sections. The book in which it appears, *Hill of Doors*, uses the imagery of houses, doors, locks and keys, and that imagery is evident in this poem – along with a strong sense of change, of movement: a turning. The "keys" here are both the keys we use to open doors and also samaras – the winged seeds of the maple – and the cover of *Hill of Doors* features a fossil samara. The lost keys that are found at the end of this poem, at the end of this year, will be useful to unlock the spring of the next.'

SOPHIE ROBINSON was born in 1985. She has an MA in Poetic Practice from Royal Holloway, University of London, and has recently completed a PhD in Queer Time and Space in Contemporary Experimental Writing. In 2011 she was Poet in Residence at the Victoria & Albert Museum. She is a lecturer in Creative Writing at Northumbria University, and divides her time between Newcastle and London. She comments, 'This was the first poem I wrote as poet in residence at the V&A in 2011. It ended up being the poem that conceptually defined the rest of the collection I produced during my residency, all of which attempted to engage with personal histories and narratives as forms of museum object-curation. In documenting important moments from a life – in this case, the breakdown of a love affair – I was attempting to treat individual histories as a kind of public archive, and by preserving them in poems I wanted to create a kind of messy institution or archive of feeling.'

CHARLOTTE RUNCIE is a former Foyle Young Poet of the Year and winner of the Christopher Tower Poetry Prize. Her work appears in anthologies *The Salt Book of Younger Poets* and *Best Scottish Poems 2011*, as well as in publications including *The Scotsman, Edinburgh Review, Magma* and *FuseLit*. She was born in 1989 and lived in Edinburgh, where she worked as a journalist; she recently moved to London. Her first pamphlet, *seventeen horse skeletons*, is published by tall-lighthouse. She writes, 'Sometimes a poem finds you. It was tempting to leave this short listing – found during some idle internet browsing for second hand furniture – as a poem in itself. But it suggested such an irresistible vignette of a night in wintry Edinburgh at the turning of the year, a missed opportunity, a girl neglected in favour of a punch-up at the bells, that I wanted to tell the story from the perspective of the other half of the "missed connection".

The poem I ended up with is an equally staccato view of that lost moment and, I hope, just as romantic in its own way, painting the small parting of two people onto the grand scenery of the city.

Most of all I wanted to write a tipsy poem in the style of the way your head sees the world after roughly four beers and a gin, when everything is tragic and profound, before the hangover kicks in and shrinks life back to how it was. It's about Edinburgh, too, a city drunk on its own rain.'

DECLAN RYAN was born in Mayo, Eire and lives in north London. His poems, reviews and essays have appeared in *Poetry Review*, *Poetry London*, *The Spectator*, *Night & Day*, *The Palm Beach Effect: Reflections on Michael Hofmann*, and elsewhere. He co-edits the *Days of Roses* anthology series and is poetry editor at *Ambit*. He comments, 'Alun Lewis was a fine poet and prose writer who served in, and died during, World War Two. While he was stationed in India he fell in love with a married woman called Freda Akroyd, communicating with her mostly by mail due to the "circumstances". The letters from Lewis to Akroyd are collected in a book called *A Cypress Walk*, and this poem is made up entirely of lines taken from those letters, not necessarily in chronological order but arranged so as – I hope – to give a sense of their relationship. The letters are extraordinary, passionate, tragic artefacts, but above all I think his poems deserve to be read more widely than they are – some, such as "Goodbye" are among my favourites of the last century. The line "I think of you all the bloody time. Do you mind?" was my spur to giving it a go – it reminded me a little of Hugo Williams, which is only ever a good thing.'

FIONA SAMPSON has published twenty-one volumes of poetry, criticism, translation and philosophy of language. She has eleven books in translation, and has received the Zlaten Prsten (Macedonia) the Charles Angoff Award (US), the Newdigate Prize, a Cholmondeley Award, awards from the Society of Authors and the Arts Councils of England and of Wales, and various PBS Recommendations. Shortlisted twice for both the T.S. Eliot Prize and Forward prizes, she is a Fellow and Council Member of the Royal Society of Literature. Her US *Selected Poems* (Sheep Meadow Press) appeared in May. She comments, 'This is one of fourteen sonnets spaced through *Coleshill*, my book about living in limestone country. Like the rest of the book, they're attempts to understand a place which I know so well that I can hardly "see" it anymore.

I've always loved the sense of two things pulling on each other in a sonnet – almost seeming to pull the poem apart – then being hauled back into congruence, if not resolution. It's the sonnet fetch, if you like: which is really a fetch and carry. In these sonnets I'm trying to sort out that pull between person and place which anyone who settles somewhere, particularly in a farming environment like Coleshill, quickly becomes aware of. The working countryside is man made; where I live affects what I do and how I feel. "The Revenant" is about this dialectic; about remembering who I was when things were different, and how that other younger self felt as she came in and out of the house where I still live. And where I'm haunted by happy memories.'

CAMELLIA STAFFORD was born in Warwickshire. She studied English Literature and Language at King's College London and has an MA in Art History from the Courtauld Institute of Art. Her debut pamphlet *another pretty colour, another break for air* was published by tall lighthouse in 2007. *Letters to the Sky*, her first collection is published by Salt. She writes, 'The title of the poem is a lyric borrowed from a Tricky song *Broken Homes* with P.J. Harvey from the *Angels with Dirty Faces* album. The song was a favourite of mine in my third year at university. I have a clear memory of sitting at the kitchen table in my shared house in East Dulwich with my friend John, who is the "you" in this poem. Following a somewhat awkward dinner party he and I had thrown for a university friend and his wife, we were listening to *Broken Homes* and I was song-speaking along.

We had cracked open another bottle of wine and begun to actually enjoy the evening, after having experienced disapproval from our friend's wife for drinking. I remember the Norwegian Cream dessert I had made was not favoured by her either. Lots of my poems draw on my friendships for inspiration. I guess this one looks at how certain friendships can be very time specific or have their most intensive periods during times of common experience. These days a few of my friendships are mainly conducted over the phone and I look back nostalgically on the years when our lives were more synchronised.'

CHLOE STOPA-HUNT is a poet and critic currently living in Cambridge. She was a Foyle Young Poet of the Year in 2003 and 2004, and won the University of Oxford's English Poem on a Sacred Subject Prize in

2011. Her poems have appeared in publications including *POEM, Oxford Poetry, Magma* and *Lung Jazz: Young British Poets for Oxfam*; she has also reviewed for *Asymptote, Mslexia, Poetry Matters* and *Poetry Review*.

She comments, 'Much of my writing in the past few years has sprung from a fascination with French history, in particular the revolutionary period, and this poem is no exception – begun in 2009, it evolved through dozens of iterations into its current form. The specificities of 1789 and 1794 have been left behind, as the poem fractures into increasingly abstract and disparate sections: underneath, I suppose the thing that caught my attention was always history itself, the slipperiness of the past, the way it gets away from you in the end. Now, this poem springs across several centuries. I'm not trying to make a point or even to tell a story, only to capture the sense of loss that attends all historical writing – or at least, all mine.'

GEORGE SZIRTES was born in Hungary and came to England as a refugee in 1956. His first book, *The Slant Door* (1979) was joint winner of the Faber Memorial Prize. He has written some dozen since. In 2004 he won the T S Eliot Prize for *Reel*, and was shortlisted for the prize again in 2009 for The Burning of the Books. In between Bloodaxe published his New and Collected Poems (2008). His most recent book is *Bad Machine*, 2013.

He comments, 'Like many poems this one starts with a perception of some coincidence, in this case between the way the lines in a poem move at the press of a key and the way time moves on with it. Time moves constantly of course, but each time it is marked by a change it becomes more real. Like many poets of a certain age I used to work on a typewriter where the end of the line was marked more physically, with the touch of the lever, the jerking back of the carriage and the whizz-chime sound as the carriage returned to position. It was the age of romantic mechanics. Could we reverse the process? Well, of course not, but I wanted to get the sense of a carriage shifting, time moving and breaking as it is embedded in the poem, the machinery of the terza rima snapped here and there by embodied fractures. Hence the violent line-breaks and, half-way through, the shift to music that too breaks and cries out while simply proceeding along a street. No one is anyone special yet everyone is. Our lives inhabit poems like crowds at individual events. So you press return and something breaks, if only a line.'

HELEN TOOKEY was born near Leicester in 1969 and currently lives in Liverpool. She has worked as a university teacher and in publishing. Her first full-length poetry collection, *Missel-Child*, is forthcoming from Carcanet in January 2014. She writes, 'The immediate inspiration for this poem was a drawing by Leonardo da Vinci that I saw in an exhibition at

Manchester Art Gallery. As a left-hander, I have always been interested in the phenomenon of *handedness*, and this drawing (the head of a young woman, in profile) struck me as very left-handed: the profile faces right, which is the way I always naturally draw faces, with my hand 'behind' the profile; and all the energy in the drawing seems to me to be moving from right to left, which is the natural direction for a left-hander when writing or drawing. In the poem I was exploring the idea of handedness in terms of space and spatial relations, partly using the image of the moon's shift of profile or orientation between waxing and waning. I also tend to see poems as themselves spaces, governed by the "grammar" of formal structuring: in this case, fourteen eight-syllable lines, so a kind of slightly narrower sonnet. Working in a sense against the formal constraints is the fact that the poem is written as one continuous sentence; I'm not sure whether I started off with that as a conscious decision or arrived at it along the way, but I can see that I was aiming at the combination of precision and fluidity that struck me so much in Leonardo's drawing.'

TIM TURNBULL was born in North Yorkshire in 1960. He worked in forestry for many years and completed the M.A. at Sheffield Hallam University in 2002. His collections 'Stranded in Sub-Atomica', 'Caligula on Ice and Other Poems' are published by Donut Press. In 2006 Turnbull was awarded the first Performance Poetry Fellowship by the Arts Foundation. He is currently working on a novel, as part of a PhD at Northumbria University.

He comments as follows, 'I was leafing through my copy of von Krafft-Ebbing's *Psychopathia Sexualis* one afternoon, as you do, when I came upon the case study from which the epigraph is taken and commenced to thinking about the way we see the objects of our affections, our beloved others, especially in the heat of desire. It put me in mind of portraits by Braque, Severini, or Picasso, which thought led me on to Picasso's African-influenced paintings. This, in turn, made me think of a fetish from sub-Saharan east Africa I'd seen in a documentary. It was a fairly unappealing little blighter, as one might say if one was a nineteenth century colonialist, and this started me musing about old horror stories (I take my spelling of Voudou from Lovecraft) wherein evil cults bring heathen curses down on barely comprehending western protagonists – all strictly Hammer and most definitely not anthropological – and how that trippy aesthetic found its way into the songs of The Cramps' *Psychedelic Jungle*, and how that psychedelic vision's fractured view of phenomena is not unlike above mentioned futuro-cubists, and the pounding rhythms of Nick and Ivy on "Voodoo Idol" gave me a hook, and I fancied myself presiding over some orgiastic and unspeakable rite and then wrote this love poem.'

MARK WALDRON was born in New York. His first collection, *The Brand New Dark*, was published by Salt in 2008, his second, *The Itchy Sea*, came out in September 2011. His work appears in *Identity Parade: New British and Irish Poets* (Bloodaxe 2010) and *Best British Poetry 2012*. He lives in east London with his wife and son.

He writes, 'This poem is one in a series about a character called (for the time being at least) Manning. He takes many forms and exists in many historical periods. In this poem he's obviously partly contemporary but he's also a zoot-suit-wearing 1940s character in occupied France as well as a jouster from the Middle Ages. In other poems he's a 15th or 16th century young man, a space explorer and a miserable stone in somebody's rock garden. There's often a Hamlet-like atmosphere surrounding him either in a sense of uncertainty and indecision or because he's acting up as an annoying lunatic. In this poem he's certainly displaying an "antic disposition", but it's also me who's in the role of Hamlet and Manning is a player who's going to receive instructions from me for his role within a poem. I want to use Manning in this instance to examine my fears about the subjects I'm drawn to and whether or not it's too exposing to voice them. The phallus is one of those subjects. For me it uniquely possesses a kind of hallucinatory quality. Also, form certain angles, it looks like the axel round which the whole happy world rotates. Manning is presenting the phallus on my behalf while I, his mortified collaborator, wring my hands off-stage.'

Originally from West Wales. NERYS WILLIAMS is the recipient of a Fulbright scholar's Award at UC Berkeley. A winner of the Ted McNulty Poetry Prize (2008) she lectures in American Literature at University College, Dublin. She has published poems and essays widely and is the author of *A Guide to Contemporary Poetry* (Edinburgh UP, 2011) as well as a study of contemporary American poetics, *Reading Error* (Peter Lang, 2007). Her first volume, *Sound Archive* (Seren, 2011), was shortlisted for the Felix Denis (Forward) prize and won the Rupert and Eithne Strong first volume prize in 2012. She is preparing her second volume, *Treasure Island*.

She comments, 'Following watching a terrific BBC 4 programme written and presented by Michael Collins *The Great Estate: the Rise and Fall of the Council House*, I became interested in Collins's research on the history of urban white working culture. His book *The Likes of Us: A Biography of the White Working Class* contains a fascinating profile of the social meetings of *The Thirteen Club*. Established in the 1880s to debunk superstitious beliefs and rituals, my own poem imagines what one of these meetings could be like. Unusually for my work at this time, the writing negotiates how the poem can somehow inhabit factual information. Written during early pregnancy (and happily a successful one) elements of superstition and ritual loomed large in my daily life. Not surprisingly, an evocation of sampled playground chants and songs feature in the poem. I am grateful to Collins's spirited evocation, which fuelled my own imagining.'

LIST OF MAGAZINES

3:AM Magazine,
www.3ammagazine.com/3am/
Editor-in-Chief: Andrew Gallix
Poetry Editor: S.J. Fowler

Cake Magazine
Dept. of English and Creative
Writing, Lancaster University,
Lancaster LA1 4YD
Editor: Martha Sprackland

Clinic, clinicpresents.com/
Editors: Sam Buchan-Watts,
Andrew Parkes, Rachael Allen,
Sean Roy Parker

Edinburgh Review, 22a Buccleuch
Place, Edinburgh EH8 9LN

Granta 12 Addison Avenue
London W11 4QR
Editor: Sigrid Rausing

Iota, PO Box 7721, Matlock
DE4 9DD
Editor: Nigel McLoughlin

Jacket jacketmagazine.com/00/
home.shtml
Editor: Michael S. Hennessey

Kaffeeklatsch manualpoetry.co.uk/
Editors: Matthew Halliday, Nadia
Connor and Joey Connolly
Lighthouse Georgian House 34
Thoroughfare, Halesworth,
Suffolk, IP19 8AP
Editor: Andrew McDonnell
Literary Review 44 Lexington
Street, London W1F 0LW
Editor: Nancy Sladek

Magma, www.magmapoetry.com/
23 Pine Walk, Carshalton
SM5 4ES

Modern Poetry in Translation
The Queens College, Oxford
OX1 4AW
Editor: Sasha Dugdale

New Walk newwalkmagazine.
wordpress.com
Editor: Rory Waterman

PN Review, Dept. of English,
University of Glasgow, 5
University Gardens, Glasgow,
G12 8QH
Editor: Michael Schmidt

Poem c/o Durham University, Department of English Studies Hallgarth House, 77 Hallgarth Street, Durham City DH1 3AY
Editor: Fiona Sampson

Poem in Which poemsinwhich. wordpress.com
Editors: Amy Key and Nia Davies

Poetry London, 81 Lambeth Walk, London SE11 6DX
Editor: Colette Bryce

Poetry Review, The Poetry Society, 22 Betterton Street, London, WC2H 9BX
Poetry Wales, 57 Nolton Street, Bridgend, Wales, CF31 3AE UK
Editor: Zoë Skoulding

Rising, 80 Cazenove Road, Stoke Newington, London, N16 6AA
Editor: Tim Wells

Shearsman, 58 Velwell Road, Exeter, EX4 4LD
Editor: Tony Frazer

Snow
Allardyce Book
14 Mount Street, Lewes, East Sussex BN7 1HL
Editors: Anthony Barnett and Ian Brinton.

The Echo Room
c/o Pighog Press, P O Box 145, Brighton, BN1 6YU
Editor: Brandan Cleary

The Erotic Review
eroticreviewmagazine.com/
Editor: editorial@ermagazine.org

The Literateur literateur.com
Editors: Kit Toda and Dan Eltringham

The Morning Star William Rust House, 52 Beachy Road, London, E3 2NS

The New Statesman 7th Floor John Carpenter House, 7 Carmelite Street, Blackfriars, London EC4Y 0AN
Editor: Jason Cowley

The Rialto, PO Box 309, Aylesham, Norwich NR11 6LN
Editor: Michael Mackmin

The White Review, www. thewhitereview.org
8th Floor, 1 Knightsbridge Green, London SW1X 7QA
Editors: Benjamin Eastham and Jacques Testard

Times Literary Supplement
3 Thomas More Square, London E98 1BS
Editor: Peter Stothard

ACKNOWLEDGEMENTS

Grateful acknowledgement is made to the publications from which the poems in this volume were chosen. Unless specifically noted otherwise, copyright to the poems is held by the individual poets.

Rachael Allen: 'Sunday' appeared in *The White Review*. Reprinted by permission of the poet.

Emily Berry: 'Arlene's House' appeared in *The Rialto* and was collected in *Dear Boy* (Faber & Faber, 2013). Reprinted by permission of the poet and the publisher.

Liz Berry: 'Bird' appeared in *Poetry London*. Reprinted by permission of the poet.

Patrick Brandon: 'The Spirit of Geometry' appeared in *Magma*. Reprinted by permission of the poet.

James Brookes: 'Amen to Artillery' appeared in *The White Review*. Reprinted by permission of the poet.

Sam Buchan-Watts: 'Nose to Tail' appeared in *Clinic*. Reprinted by permission of the poet.

Hayley Buckland: 'Supper' appeared in *Lighthouse*. Reprinted by permission of the poet.

Harry Burke: 'realspace' appeared in *Clinic*. Reprinted by permission of the poet.

John Burnside: 'At the Entering of the New Year' appeared in *Times Literary Supplement*. Reprinted by permission of the poet.

Matthew Caley: 'My Beloved' appeared in *The Echo Room*. Reprinted by permission of the poet.

Niall Campbell: 'On Eriskay' appeared in *Granta*. Reprinted by permission of the poet.

Ian Cartland: 'Six Winters' appeared in *Poetry London*. Reprinted by permission of the poet.

Melanie Challenger: 'The Daffodil' appeared in *Poetry London*. Reprinted by permission of the poet.

Kayo Chingonyi: 'from calling a spade a spade' appeared in *Poetry Review*. Reprinted by permission of the poet.

John Clegg: 'Figtree' appeared in *The White Review*. Reprinted by permission of the poet.

David Constantine: 'Foxes, rain' appeared in *Poetry London*. Reprinted by permission of the poet.

Emily Critchley: 'Some Curious Things II' appeared in *Poetry Wales*. Reprinted by permission of the poet.

Claire Crowther: 'Trompe l'oeil' appeared in *Shearsman*. Reprinted by permission of the poet.

Francine Elena: 'Ode to a 1980s Baton Twirling World Champion' appeared in *3:AM Magazine*. Reprinted by permission of the poet.

Menna Elfyn: 'Babysitting in the *Crematorium*. Reprinted by permission of the poet.

Carco yn y Crem' appeared in *Mslexia*. Reprinted by permission of the poet.

Leontia Flynn: 'MacNeice's Mother' appeared in *Poetry London*. Reprinted by permission of the poet.

Charlotte Geater: 'avoid using the word 'pussy'' appeared in *Clinic*. Reprinted by permission of the poet.

Dai George: 'Seven Rounds with Bill's Ghost' appeared in *Poetry Wales*. Reprinted by permission of the poet.

Matthew Gregory: 'A Room in Taiwan, 2010' appeared in *Poetry Review*. Reprinted by permission of the poet.

Philip Gross: 'The Works' appeared in *Magma* and was collected in *Later* (Bloodaxe Books, 2013). Reprinted by permission of the poet and the publisher.

David Harsent: 'Effaced' appeared in *Poem*. Reprinted by permission of the poet.

Stuart Henson: 'The Builder' appeared in *Modern Poetry in Translation*. Reprinted by permission of the poet.

Wayne Holloway-Smith: 'Poem in Which' appeared in *Poem in Which*. Reprinted by permission of the poet.

Sarah Howe: 'Scrying: turpentine' appeared in *PN Review*. Reprinted by permission of the poet.

A.B. Jackson: 'from Natural History' appeared in *Poetry Review*. Reprinted by permission of the poet.

Andrew Jamison: 'What I'll Say When I Get Back' appeared in *Edinburgh Review*. Reprinted by permission of the poet.

Alan Jenkins: 'Sea-Music' appeared in *New Walk*. Reprinted by permission of the poet.

Chris McCabe: 'The Alchemist' appeared in *Poetry Review*. Reprinted by permission of the poet.

John McCullough: '!' appeared in *Poetry London*. Reprinted by permission of the poet.

Patrick McGuinness: 'Doors and Windows of Wallonia' appeared in *Literary Review*. Reprinted by permission of the poet.

Edward Mackay: 'Afterword' appeared in *Shearsman*. Reprinted by permission of the poet.

Andrew McMillan: 'if it wasn't for the nights' appeared in *The Rialto*. Reprinted by permission of the poet.

Kona Macphee: 'Mind' appeared in *Iota*. Reprinted by permission of the poet.

Allison McVety: 'Finlandia' appeared in *Poetry London*. Reprinted by permission of the poet.

D.S. Marriott: 'The Redeemers' appeared in *Snow*. Reprinted by permission of the poet.

Glyn Maxwell: 'Christmas Seven Times Seven' appeared in *Times Literary Supplement* and was collected in *Pluto* (Picador, 2013). Reprinted by permission of the poet and the publisher.

Christopher Middleton: 'The Ghosting Of Paul Celan' appeared in *Poetry Review*. Reprinted by permission of the poet.

Kate Miller: 'Salvage' appeared in *Time Literary Supplement*. Reprinted by permission of the poet.

Helen Mort: 'Admit you feel like all the ice skates in Brazil' appeared in *Poetry London*. Reprinted by permission of the poet.

Alistair Noon' 'from Earth Records, 27' appeared in *The Morning Star*. Reprinted by permission of the poet.

Richard O'Brien: 'So Much Will Waste' appeared in *The Erotic Review*. Reprinted by permission of the poet.

Sean O'Brien: 'Thirteen O'Clocks' appeared in *Poem*. Reprinted by permission of the poet.

Richard Osmond: 'The Well' appeared in *The Literateur*. Reprinted by permission of the poet.

Ruth Padel: 'from The Okazaki Fragments' appeared in *Poem*. Reprinted by permission of the poet.

Rebecca Perry: 'Pow' appeared in *Poetry London*. Reprinted by permission of the poet.

Pascale Petit: 'Sainte-Chapelle' appeared in *Poetry London*. Reprinted by permission of the poet.

Heather Phillipson: 'Rumination on 25mm of Cotton' appeared in *Poetry London*. Reprinted by permission of the poet.

Jody Porter: 'Girl at the World's End' appeared in *Rising*. Reprinted by permission of the poet.

Kate Potts: 'Thirty-three' appeared in *Poetry Review*. Reprinted by permission of the poet.

Sam Riviere: 'No Touching' appeared in *Clinic*. Reprinted by permission of the poet.

Michael Symmons Roberts: 'After a Line by George Seferis' appeared in *The Rialto* and was collected in *Drysalter* (Jonathan Cape, 2013). Reprinted by permission of the poet and the publisher.

Robin Robertson: 'Finding the Keys' appeared in *Poetry London* and was collected in *Hill of Doors* (Picador, 2013). Reprinted by permission of the poet and the publisher.

Sophie Robinson: 'nsfw' appeared in *Jacket* and collected in *The Institute of Our Love in Disrepair* (Bad Press, 2012). Reprinted by permission of the poet.

Charlotte Runcie: 'Lothian Road, Saturday Night' appeared in *Edinburgh Review*. Reprinted by permission of the poet.

Declan Ryan: 'From Alun Lewis' appeared in *Poetry Review*. Reprinted by permission of the poet.

Fiona Sampson: 'The Revenant' appeared in *The New Statesman* and was collected in *Coleshill* (Chatto & Windus, 2013) Reprinted by permission of the poet and the publisher.

Camellia Stafford: 'I will stay at home and talk on the telephone' appeared in *Magma*. Reprinted by permission of the poet.

Chloe Stopa-Hunt: 'The Paris Poems' appeared in *Cake*. Reprinted by permission of the poet.

George Szirtes: 'Songlines' appeared in *Kaffeeklatsch*. Reprinted by permission of the poet.

Helen Tookey: 'Portrait of a Young Woman' appeared in *Poetry Wales*. Reprinted by permission of the poet.

Tim Turnbull: 'Fetish' appeared in *Rising*. Reprinted by permission of the poet.

Mark Waldron: 'Collaboration' appeared in *Kaffeeklatsch*. Reprinted by permission of the poet.

Nerys Williams: 'The Thirteen Club' appeared in *Poetry Wales*. Reprinted by permission of the poet.